The Weiser Field Guide to
the paranormal

Abductions, Apparitions, ESP, Synchronicity, and More
Unexplained Phenomena from Other Realms

Judith Joyce

WEISER BOOKS
San Francisco, CA / Newburyport, MA

First published in 2010 by
Red Wheel/Weiser, LLC
With offices at:
500 Third Street, Suite 230
San Francisco, CA 94107
www.redwheelweiser.com

Library of Congress Cataloging-in-Publication Data
Joyce, Judith, 1960–
The Weiser field guide to the paranormal : abductions,
apparitions, ESP, synchronicity, and more unexplained phenomena from
other realms / by Judith Joyce.
p. cm.
Includes bibliographical references.
ISBN 978-1-57863-488-0 (alk. paper)
1. Parapsychology. I. Title. II.
Title: Field guide to the paranormal.
BF1031.J74 2010
130.3--dc22   2010036790

Cover and text design by Sara Gillingham
Cover photo ©Todd Warnock/Getty Images

Printed in Canada
TCP
10 9 8 7 6 5 4 3 2 1

Acknowledgments

My thanks to Jan Johnson, Amber Guetebier, Michael Kerber, Sara Gillingham, Susie Pitzen, Dennis Fitzgerald, and Laurie Trufant of Weiser Books, as well as Clare Asch, Greg Brandenburgh, Sherri Devereau, Johannes Gårdbäck, Judika Illes, and Robert Murch.

Contents

Introduction

Can everything be explained? That is the question that ultimately lies at the heart of paranormal mysteries.

The paranormal is defined as events, experiences, beings, or things for which there is no scientific evidence or explanation—at least, not yet. Among the topics classified as paranormal are ghosts, psychic abilities, extraterrestrials, and unidentified creatures. The paranormal encompasses the most profound mysteries of the universe:

- What happens after death?
- Is there an immortal soul?
- Can the living communicate with the dead and vice versa?
- Do some individuals possess special powers and abilities that others do not?
- Is there life beyond Earth?
- Do beings from other planets or dimensions walk among us?
- Are provable facts the only reality?

The word *paranormal* first emerged in the English language during the 1920s. The dictionary defines paranormal as "supernatural," something beyond normal occurrences and situations. The prefix *para-* derives from a Greek word and has various meanings, including "beside," "beyond," "closely related," "abnormal," and "faulty."

Once upon a time, events like ghost sightings were considered "normal." Ghosts and strange psychic abilities may not have been looked upon with favor, but they were accepted as natural. Not every ghost sighting was accepted as true, but few doubted that hauntings could and did occur. You might have been burned as a witch for demonstrating telekinesis or clairvoyance, but no one doubted that these powers existed. Although what happens after death was subject to fierce theological dispute, most people believed that an eternal undying soul existed. Few scoffed at the idea—or at least not until a massive change in societal perceptions began during the 18th century with the flowering of the Age of Reason.

During the Age of Reason, the way people thought was transformed, as were the topics they thought about. Concepts and phenomena previously accepted without question were now closely considered and analyzed. It was the beginning of a new age that revered rational thought as opposed to the faith prized by earlier generations. Myth busters emerged who questioned deeply held beliefs and demanded evidence and proof. A best-selling pamphlet, *The Age of Reason* by American author and revolutionary Thomas Paine (1737–1809), radically challenged organized religion and the Bible's validity, giving the era its name. Of course, the Church fought back, accusing people of worshipping reason and rationality as if they were gods.

The scientific method now taught in every Western school—a method crucial to modern research and thinking—was formalized during this era, although its roots stretch back into antiquity. The scientific method is a system involving a series of clearly defined and mandatory steps. First, a hypothesis—an assumption or statement to be proved or disproved—is made. Then the hypothesis is tested through experiments designed to obtain clear, scientific results that either support or negate it. For the hypothesis to be considered true, these results must be reproducible by other researchers. Since this method acknowledges only events, beings, experiences, and phenomena that are standardized and predictable, you can already see the problem it presents when it comes to the *para*normal.

An example of an easy-to-prove hypothesis is: "If I touch a lit match to a piece of paper, the paper will burn." The statement "Ghosts do exist," on the other hand, is a challenging and difficult hypothesis to prove. Paranormal beings and experiences are rarely predictable, or standardized, or easily controlled through experiments.

The paranormal encompasses many unique one-time events, as well as experiences like UFO sightings or alien abductions that are reported more frequently, but with a wide degree of variation. Are any of these reports true? Or is everyone who describes these experiences invariably wrong, misguided—or worse, a hoaxer? *Can* the existence of ghosts be proven scientifically? So far, ghosts and their paranormal compatriots, extraterrestrials, have consistently defied the scientific method, but does this lack of proof conclusively establish that they *don't* exist?

In fact, many do believe that anything that cannot be proven and established scientifically is, by definition, false, and that those who claim otherwise are lying, mistaken, or mentally ill. And yet . . .

Centuries after the dawning of the Age of Reason, people continue to report strange experiences and weird phenomena. According to a 2009 Pew Forum survey, 29 percent of all Americans claim to have felt in touch with someone who was already dead; 18 percent say they have seen or been in the presence of ghosts; 24 percent believe in reincarnation. In 2002, the Sci Fi Channel, an American cable television network, reported that a whopping 72 percent of Americans believe that the government is not revealing everything it knows about UFOs. According to a 1997 survey, almost three million Canadians claim to have witnessed UFOs. Are all these individuals lying or wrong?

Complicating the issue is the fact that not everything that can't be proven conclusively is classified as paranormal. Dark matter, for example, is a respectable "scientific theory," while ball lightning is considered "paranormal."

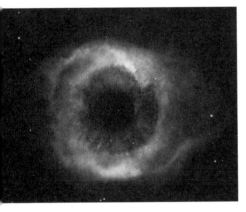

These distinctions are more than just semantics; they influence what is studied and what is not. Scientists are subjected to ridicule or worse if they appear to take anything classified as paranormal seriously—for example, if they study ghosts or UFOs, they are likely to lose research funding or fail to receive tenure.

Paranormal topics evoke powerful emotions and, often, knee-jerk reactions. Some passionately insist on the validity of paranormal experiences even when faced with obvious fraud. Others take the opposite tack, insisting that paranormal events simply cannot be real, regardless of evidence. Renowned UFO researcher Budd Hopkins asks us to consider exactly who are the true believers and who are the skeptics—those willing to accept that something out of the ordinary just *might* be true—versus those who deny this possibility simply because they believe it *can't* be true.

Beginning in the late 19th century, various paranormal societies were founded as forums where people would share their alleged experiences and investigate the validity of the claims. Now, at the start of the 21st century, the paranormal is an international entertainment sensation. Films, video games, television series, and best-selling books all feature paranormal activity. It is still, however, impossible to overestimate the influence of the Age of Reason on these topics. Many of the firmest proponents of the reality of the paranormal seek evidence that will conclusively provide scientific proof. They attempt to use scientific technology to provide this proof—so far to no avail—claiming that perhaps all that is lacking are the correct tools. After all, no one now disputes the existence of radiation, which remained undiscovered until the very last years of the 19th century.

In 1768, the French Academy of Science requested that renowned scientist Antoine Lavoisier investigate reports of a huge stone that had fallen from the sky and embedded itself in the Earth. Lavoisier was utterly convinced that the great stone simply could not have fallen from the sky and insisted that witnesses were either mistaken or lying. It was another fifty years before meteorites were accepted and recognized officially by science. New technology emerges at an ever-increasing pace, and perhaps, someday, it will be possible to prove definitively whether or not paranormal activity truly exists. In the meantime, here is *The Weiser Field Guide to the Paranormal* to help you explore and investigate some of the world's strangest phenomena and most profound mysteries.

Consider these questions: Can the souls of the deceased appear to their loved ones or even call them on the telephone? What about alien abductions? Does the *chupacabra*, a blood-sucking predator, really exist? Is there such a thing as telepathy or clairsentience, and how can you recognize these supernatural powers if you have them? Within these pages, you will meet many of the pioneers of paranormal research, learn about some of the most mysterious stars of the paranormal firmament, and discover paranormal societies and haunted sites where you can experience the paranormal for yourself. Make up your own mind with the help of *The Weiser Field Guide to the Paranormal*.

The Weiser Field Guide
to the Paranormal

Akashic Records

The Akashic Records are a compendium of knowledge said to exist on an astral or nonphysical plane. The term *Akashic* derives from a Sanskrit word meaning "sky," "space," or "ether." The Akashic Records are thus envisioned as a cosmic library containing records of everything that has ever occurred anywhere—including thoughts and feelings. Anything you or anyone else has ever thought, dreamt, or experienced throughout time is preserved forever in the Akashic Records.

Jane Roberts, channeling the entity known as Seth, claimed that an idea, once conceived, exists forever. Thus anything you need or desire to know—literally anything, even things that are hypothetically impossible to know—can be found within the Akashic Records. Methods of accessing these records include mediumship and hypnosis.

Alien

The meaning of the word "alien" varies depending on context. According to the dictionary, the word means "strange," "foreign," "belonging or owing allegiance to another country or government," or "differing in nature or character typically to the point of incompatibility." In standard everyday usage, the word usually refers to residents of a nation who are not citizens—for instance, "alien workers" or "illegal aliens." If someone is identified as an alien in a news article, most likely the reference is to a human lacking the required documentation. In the language of the paranormal, however, "alien" is a synonym for "extraterrestrial"—life-forms that are not native to Earth.

The way people use the word "alien" may reveal their attitudes. The nuance or undercurrent implicit in the word tends to be one of fear or hostility, at least when it isn't mockery. People make jokes about aliens from outer space or they report horrific alien abductions. By contrast, those who consider these beings benevolent rarely use the word "alien" when referring to them, preferring neutral terms like "extraterrestrial" or friendly ones like "space brethren" and "visitors." Ufologist Budd Hopkins, who considers aliens predatory, suggests that they should be called intruders.

Alien Abduction

If aliens are visiting our planet, why are they here? What is their motivation? What do they want? Answers to these questions may lie in testimony given by countless people from all over the globe who claim they have been abducted forcibly by aliens, sometimes repeatedly and over extended periods of time. Alien abduction is also known as *abduction phenomenon*. The first widely publicized case was that of Barney and Betty Hill.

The standard term for an abduction victim is *abductee*; however, some prefer to be called *experiencers*. Although experiences vary—with most described as traumatic, some as neutral, and a few as pleasurable—abduction researchers have discovered commonalities among many testimonials.

Most abduction reports describe individuals who are taken aboard an alien spacecraft, where they are usually subjected to forced physical examinations, especially of the reproductive system. Some claim that aliens harvest human eggs, sperm, or even fetuses. Others claim that skin and hair samples are taken. Yet others claim that tracking devices are implanted in the human body.

Most abductees are eventually returned, typically back to the place where they were abducted. Although these are frequently public places, abductions and returns tend to be unnoticed by bystanders. (Exceptions do exist.) Some suggest that extraterrestrials may possess sophisticated cloaking technology that creates temporary invisibility shields.

Following their return, many abductees experience "missing-time syndrome," which is a form of post-traumatic amnesia. They may notice odd things: their watches have stopped working or their clothing is inexplicably torn; jewelry or other items may be missing and later mysteriously returned. Some discover strange scoop-shaped scars on their bodies, especially on their legs.

Alien abductions may be more common than is actually reported. Some believe that many who experience abductions lack conscious recall of the event. In other words, just because you don't remember being abducted by an alien doesn't mean it didn't happen. Many who do recall encounters may be hesitant to describe experiences, fearing ridicule or accusations of mental illness. Others will not come forward because their captors have advised them not to do so and they are afraid.

Abductions may not be random. Abducted children report being told to expect future visits. Like human child molesters, aliens allegedly warn children not to tell their parents of their experiences, or else...

Whether or not an actual abduction is remembered, many abductees share common experiences— for example, extreme anxiety, especially of medical procedures. Many have recurrent disturbing dreams or nightmares with motifs that include weird aircraft, medical exams, running, escaping, or being captured. Some experience flashbacks during waking hours. Many develop a sudden and sometimes inexplicable interest in UFOs, including a compulsion to learn more about them. Some abductees develop health problems, although others experience miraculous healings of pre-existing conditions and illnesses.

Mainstream science dismisses the literal validity of abduction claims, attributing them instead to false-memory syndrome, mental illness, or attention-seeking fraud.

Theories differ as to why aliens abduct humans. The most malevolent suggest that aliens are studying us in order to enslave us more easily. Others claim they seek to create transgenic beings, hybrid human-aliens, who will live discreetly among us and insidiously and gradually conquer Earth. Could it not also be true that these technologically advanced aliens are just scientists seeking pure knowledge?

Those perceiving extraterrestrials as benevolent suggest that they wish to preserve the human race. After all, we tag endangered animals and subject them to DNA testing. We store the DNA of endangered animals in order to protect them against extinction. Perhaps aliens consider *us* endangered and desire only to prevent our extinction.

Alien Encounters

Not all alien encounters involve abduction. Testimonials from those who claim to have encountered extraterrestrials range from accounts of horrific abduction to statements of gratitude for having met such spiritually evolved and technologically advanced beings. Since 1972, sightings and encounters have been classified as seven types:

- Close Encounters of the First Kind involve sighting a UFO.
- Close Encounters of the Second Kind involve discovering evidence of UFOs or extraterrestrials.
- Close Encounters of the Third Kind involve sighting extraterrestrials or simple contact with them.
- Close Encounters of the Fourth Kind are alien abductions.
- Close Encounters of the Fifth Kind involve continuous communication and the potential formation of a relationship between alien and human. The human is more than the equivalent of a laboratory animal. The alien may serve as the equivalent of a spirit guide and may be described as entirely benevolent.
- Close Encounters of the Sixth Kind involve the death of a human being or a terrestrial animal, such as a cow, during an alien encounter.
- Close Encounters of the Seventh Kind involve genetic interchange between humans and aliens and the creation of hybrid or transgenic beings.

Alix de Telieux

The modern Spiritualist movement was born in 1848 when the Fox sisters of Hydesville, New York allegedly communicated with a spirit via rapping and knocking. Young Maggie Fox is usually credited with spontaneously inventing this system. Although it is highly unlikely that Maggie or anyone in the Fox family was aware of it, in fact, this type of mystical rapping was not a unique phenomenon. Over the centuries, similar experiences had been recounted. The best documented is the 16th-century haunting of the convent of St. Pierre de Lyons in France.

In 1522, Alix de Telieux, a young novice, ran away from this convent, absconding with some jewels. She was reported to be living a dissolute life, and a few years later, the convent heard reports that she had died, possibly in 1524. In 1528, another young nun, Anthoinette de

Grollée, who had been Alix's friend when she was at the convent, began hearing mysterious sounds in her room, as if someone were rapping loudly on the floor with their knuckles, although no one was there. The rapping was ignored at first, in hopes that it would go away, but it did not. Instead, it grew louder and more continuous. As with the Fox sisters, this disembodied rapping was not isolated to Anthoinette's room, but followed her throughout the convent. Other nuns heard it as well.

Eventually, the convent's mother superior felt obliged to notify the bishop. He dispatched a priest, Adrian de Montalambert, to investigate. Montalambert heard the rapping and, convinced that it was Alix, tried to communicate with her. He decided to ask the spirit questions that it could answer with a predetermined, codified number of raps—one for yes, two for no, and so forth. Once the system was established, the ghost became extremely communicative, even chatty. The spirit confirmed that it was indeed Alix and said that she had obtained a reprieve from purgatory in order to seek salvation. She gave the priest the sordid details of her life, confessed her sins, and begged for absolution. She requested that arrangements be made for her corpse to be exhumed and reburied in the convent. Only then, she claimed, could she rest in peace.

The request was granted. Alix was given a funeral appropriate to a nun in good standing. For a few days afterward, all was quiet, but the spirit's final departure was dramatic. The rapping abruptly returned—this time in the form of loud, constant drumming. Father Montalambert returned to the convent and reestablished contact. As the spirit announced that Alix had been released from purgatory and was en route to heaven, Anthoinette was seen to be levitating.

Suddenly, there was a huge thud similar to the sound of a massive hammer. Witnesses heard the sound of thirty-three distinct and loud blows accompanied by the sudden appearance of a light so blindingly, dazzlingly bright that no one could see. (In Christian context, the number thirty-three has tremendous significance as the age Christ reputedly attained before the Crucifixion.) Following these thirty-three thuds, the noise stopped, the light went out, and Anthoinette tumbled to the ground. The rapping ceased forever.

Apparition

You clearly see someone standing before you . . . until suddenly the being vanishes into thin air or walks through a wall. You see a dazzlingly beautiful woman standing on a cloud, but when you attempt to discuss this strange sighting with others standing nearby, you realize that you are the only one who can see her. Or perhaps the entire crowd does see her . . . until she too vanishes into thin air. These are classic examples of apparitions.

An apparition is the paranormal appearance of someone who is not alive (such as a ghost), not human (such as a spirit), or a living human being who is not physically present. Some ghosts appear as apparitions, but an apparition is not necessarily a ghost. By definition, an apparition *must* be visual. Without exception, apparitions are seen. Paranormal phenomena that are heard—a poltergeist's rapping or a ghost clanking its chains—are not apparitions, unless there is also a visual component.

Some apparitions interact with those who witness them while others do not. Regardless, an apparition is *substantial;* it appears to be physically present, not merely seen in the mind's eye. Some apparitions look extremely normal, nothing in their appearance indicating that they are paranormal. For example, you open your front door to discover a friend or neighbor standing there. You may speak with each other, or the person may be oddly silent. Nothing seems paranormal until, hours later, you discover that your visitor was actually miles away at the time or no longer among the living. Other apparitions are instantly recognizable as paranormal—for example, transparent ghosts or fantastic creatures.

Apparitions of the dead or dying may be accompanied by drops in temperature or cold spots. They may also be accompanied by auras or vividly bright light. The most famous fictional apparitions are the ghosts of Christmas Past, Present, and Future in Charles Dickens' story, *A Christmas Carol.*

The most famous apparitions are the so-called Marian apparitions—visions identified as the Virgin Mary. Although some have been dismissed as illusions, the Vatican asserts the validity of many, including those that occurred in Knock, Ireland; Fatima, Portugal; Lourdes, France; and in Medjugorge, previously in Yugoslavia, but now within the borders of Bosnia-Herzegovina. The most renowned occurred on Tepeyac Hill near Mexico City, where the apparition now known as the Lady of Guadalupe was first witnessed on December 12, 1531. The basilica built on that site is the most visited Roman Catholic shrine in the world, the annual pilgrimage celebrating the anniversary of that apparition attended by millions. Over six million pilgrims were there in December 2009.

⌁⌁⌁ Apparition, Crisis ⌁⌁⌁

A crisis apparition is a very specific type of apparition in which the person witnessed is later discovered to be someone who could *not* have been there because he or she had just died or was dying. There are various theories put forward to explain crisis apparitions. For example, one suggests that when someone is near death or in the throes of extreme trauma, they are somehow able to send a message telepathically to someone with whom they share strong bonds. Another claims that, at the moment of death, it somehow becomes possible for the dying to project an apparition of themselves. A related phenomenon may be phone calls from the dead.

Many cases of crisis apparitions have been reported, but in general, they are difficult to verify, as the person witnessing the apparition is usually alone at the time. A famous exception involves the case of eighteen-year-old British Royal Air Force pilot, David McConnell. On December 7, 1918, McConnell was ordered to fly his plane from the base at Scampton, Lincolnshire to another at Tadcaster. He left at 11:30 A.M., telling his roommate, Lieutenant Larkin, that he would take the train back, expecting to return later in the afternoon.

At 3:25 P.M., Larkin was reading in the room they shared when he heard footsteps approaching. McConnell opened the door, still wearing his flying uniform and holding his flight helmet in his left hand. The men greeted each other and spoke briefly, then McConnell left, shutting the door behind him. Larkin heard footsteps receding and assumed that McConnell had gone to file his flight report or have tea.

Twenty minutes later, another lieutenant came to their room, wanting to know when McConnell, with whom he had plans for that night, would return. Larkin told him that McConnell had already returned, but the other man was adamant that he had not. They went to search for him together and discovered that McConnell had, in fact, *not* reported back, and that the front gate guard had not seen him. They continued searching . . . . His plane had crashed and he had died at 3:25 P.M., the time when Larkin reported seeing him. The case is considered unusual because, although only one person witnessed the apparition, Larkin reported seeing McConnell to several people, describing exactly what he had witnessed before he could possibly have known of the plane crash.

Apport

An *apport* is an object that mysteriously and miraculously appears in a closed area—for example, a room in which a séance is being held. The object just materializes as if out of thin air. A classic example is the sudden materialization of a vase of flowers or a trumpet. However, any sort of object may materialize, from the tiniest jewel to massive blocks of ice. The word itself derives from the French *apporter*, "to bring." Thus apports may be understood as gifts or messages from spirits. Apports are considered examples of physical mediumship.

An *asport* is an apport in reverse—an object that mysteriously disappears from a closed area and miraculously materializes elsewhere. For example, a vase filled with roses may disappear from a room in which a séance is being held only to rematerialize spontaneously in another room miles away.

Area 51

Nickname for a United States military base located in southern Nevada, approximately eighty-three miles from Las Vegas. Another nickname for the base is Dreamland. Area 51 is located within the Nevada Test and Training

Range complex, hidden in the mountains around Groom Lake, one of many dry lakebeds in the region. It is estimated to have an area of approximately 575 square miles. Area 51 is so top secret that it does not appear on U.S. Geological Survey maps or on aviation charts.

Although Area 51 is a restricted area, totally off limits to the public, it is the subject of much fascination, speculation, and rumor. A mecca for UFO enthusiasts, it is contained in a valley ringed by mountain ranges that make it virtually impossible to get close enough to see. To describe the area as remote and harsh is an understatement. To reach the closest vantage point, Tikaboo Peak, approximately twenty-six miles from the base, requires some hiking and steep mountain climbing. Temperatures in the region are extreme, ranging from thirty below zero in the winter to 110 degrees in the shade during summer months.

Those who trespass into Area 51 are detained, arrested, and fined between $650 and $5,000, depending on circumstances. Jail sentences of up to six months may also be imposed. Guards are allegedly authorized to shoot intruders on sight.

Founded in 1955 to test the newly developed U2 spy plane, the base has since been expanded and used for many other projects—for example, the development and testing of the B-2 stealth bomber. Because of the exceptionally high security maintained, combined with the remote location, little if anything is really known about activities at Area 51. Some ufologists claim that ongoing research on alien technology is conducted there. There are also rumors of an extensive network of underground tunnels beneath the complex. Unusual nocturnal celestial activity has been reported in proximity to Area 51, including many alleged UFO sightings. The best, most accessible views are found along the Extraterrestrial Highway.

Atlantis

Do the remains of a destroyed continent lie at the bottom of the sea? Needless to say, as this is a book on the paranormal, no conclusive evidence has yet been recovered. However, the topic of the lost continent of Atlantis has enthralled people for literally thousands of years. Over 2,000 books have been written about Atlantis, with more undoubtedly on the way.

The first documented reference to Atlantis comes from the Greek philosopher Plato in his book *Timaeus*, written in approximately 355 B.C.E. Every other account relies to a varying extent on Plato's. The philosopher claimed to have heard legends of Atlantis from descendants of the Greek poet and lawgiver Solon (c. 638 B.C.E.–c. 558 B.C.E.), who learned of it from Egyptian high priests. The information was passed down through Solon's family. Plato estimated that Atlantis was destroyed 9,000 years before his own time, offering two

dates for this cataclysm, now calcu-
lated as 8570 B.C.E. and 9421 B.C.E.

For centuries, Atlantis allegedly
dominated the Atlantic, as well as
parts of what Plato called "the opposite continent." Some speculate that
this refers to the Americas, although
others believe it indicates islands off
the western Atlantic coasts of Europe
or Africa. Plato describes Atlantis as "vast," but whether
he meant the island itself or its empire is unclear.

According to Plato, Atlantis was founded by
Poseidon, the powerful sea deity. Poseidon fathered
five sets of twins. The eldest son was Atlas, and the
continent as well as its surrounding ocean was named
for him. Poseidon divided Atlantis into ten sections,
each to be ruled first by one of his children and then
by their heirs. An architectural marvel, Atlantis
contained concentric walls and canals with a high
hill in the center, topped by a shrine housing a solid
gold statue of Poseidon. The Atlanteans were allegedly a very highly evolved people, both spiritually and
technologically.

There are different versions of what led to
Atlantis' doom. The simplest is that Atlantis was the
victim of straightforward natural disasters—a series
of incredibly potent earthquakes accompanied by
devastating tsunamis. Other versions claim that these
earthquakes were no accident, that Atlantis became

corrupt and tyrannical and that its domination of the Mediterranean became too much for ancient Greeks, who rose up in rebellion, defeating the Atlanteans in a pivotal naval battle. Simultaneously, responding to Greek prayers, Zeus punished the Atlanteans by striking them with storms, floods, earthquakes, and tidal waves, causing the whole continent to sink beneath the seas. Yet another explanation suggests that Atlantis was responsible for its own destruction— that, too advanced for their own good, the Atlanteans developed a doomsday technology, possibly nuclear, that caused its destruction.

According to prophet Edgar Cayce, the Atlanteans constructed sophisticated power plants with giant laser-like crystals, with ultimately disastrous results. Although Atlantis was wiped off the face of the Earth, he claimed, some Atlanteans survived. Cayce said that the nearly universal tales of a cataclysmic deluge, like the biblical story of Noah's ark, are vestigial memories of Atlantis. Many Atlanteans, he said, were able to escape to Egypt and elsewhere before the great island sank. According to Cayce, the souls of many Atlanteans have reincarnated in our present time as humanity faces many of the same issues once faced by Atlantis.

The location of this fabled continent is controversial. Plato's report has it in the Atlantic Ocean, just off the coast of Africa. Others place Atlantis in the Mediterranean or Caribbean seas. Cayce claimed that Atlantis extended from the Azores to the Bahamas and said that it would arise again in either 1968 or 1969, a prediction since proved incorrect. His prediction does correspond, however, to the discovery of the controversial Bimini Road, an underwater rock formation in the Bahamas. Some consider this road a remnant of Atlantis and thus at least a partial fulfillment of Cayce's prophesy.

Automatic Writing

Have you ever written or typed words that you didn't intend to write or type? Then you have engaged in automatic writing, among the most common paranormal phenomena. Many do it accidentally on occasion, but some are able to harness this skill in order to communicate with spirits or probe their own subconscious.

Automatic writing occurs without using the conscious mind. In other words, your mind does not control the actions of your hands. Automatic writing may be produced while in a trance or in a conscious state or any place in between. Hypnotism is sometimes used to facilitate automatic writing. Usually pen and paper are used, but automatic writing may also be done with chalk and slate, or even with a typewriter, a computer, or any device that involves writing.

With automatic writing, *something* guides the human hand to produce words, but what is it? Depending on circumstances and the person doing the writing, it may have different sources. The impetus toward automatic writing may come from within the hidden human psyche, or it may be derived externally. Spirits, for instance, may use a human body to deliver messages.

Automatic writing enables subconscious knowledge to break through the barriers of consciousness. Words produced automatically may express either the subconscious or the intuitive self. Sit quietly with pen and paper. Hold the pen poised over the paper but do not consciously write. It may take a little while, but eventually you may be surprised to discover that, without knowing it, you have written something on the paper.

Automatic writing is considered a form of channeling or mediumship. Spirits "speak" through a person's hands rather than through the mouth. Automatic writing may be quite different from a person's regular writing. It may produce unfamiliar handwriting and may be done at great speed without pause for thought. Famed Boston medium Lenore Piper was able to write with both hands while simultaneously carrying on a conversation. Each of the three was completely distinct, her two hands and her mouth acting independently of each other.

Often, information conveyed via automatic writing is beyond the knowledge or even comprehension of the person doing the writing. People may write in alphabets or languages that they don't know. This art of writing in a language not consciously known is called *xenoglossy*. Some believe this to be indicative of spirit communications—an English-speaking medium may channel the words of a Croatian-speaking ghost, for instance—while others believe that this reveals otherwise repressed past-life memories. In this life, you may only understand English, but in a previous one, perhaps you spoke Russian and somewhere in the deepest recesses of your mind still do. Automatic writing allows these memories to surface.

Automatic writing harnesses the act of writing to communicate with other realms. Contactee Frances Swan claimed to channel telepathic communications from the commanders of two alien spaceships in automatic writing sessions that lasted from one to five hours each.

An example of automatic writing appears in the 1980 film, *The Changeling*.

 Baba Vanga

Known as the Bulgarian Oracle, Vangelia Pandeva Gushterova (née Dimitrova), born January 31, 1911, was a blind clairvoyant, healer, herbalist, visionary, and mystic who has been compared to the prophet Nostradamus. Many are convinced that she possessed paranormal powers.

In Slavic traditions, *baba* is a term of affection and respect for an older woman, while *Vanga* is the diminutive form of *Vangelia*, a name related to the word "evangelist," which itself derives from a Greek root word meaning "good news." And good news is what Baba Vanga preferred to deliver. She spent much of her life in mountainous southwest Bulgaria, a region dotted with numerous thermal hot springs reputed to have curative properties. Hundreds of people visited her daily, hoping for prophetic information and healing.

Born to an impoverished family, Baba Vanga was a frail premature baby, not expected to survive. When she was twelve, a whirlwind lifted the thin girl into the air, dumping her in a field. It took some time before she was located. When finally found, Vanga's eyes were covered with dust and debris, and she was unable to open them without excruciating pain. Soon, her eyesight began to fail. No remedies helped. In 1925, she was sent to a school for the blind in what is now Serbia, where she learned to read Braille, although she was never more than semiliterate.

Baba Vanga claimed that it was after she lost her vision that she received her powers of clairvoyance, which first became apparent when, despite her blindness and from a distance, she located a sheep that her father, a shepherd, had lost. She said that she could "see" it. Rumors of her gift spread, attracting many who sought her help. Although her reputation derived originally from her accurate prophesies, Baba Vanga was also a healer who prescribed herbal and floral cures.

Her psychic skills attracted a husband. On May 10, 1942, Vanga married Dimitar Gushterov whom she had met when he came to ask her to reveal the identity of his brother's killer. (She made him promise not to seek vengeance before she would tell him.)

Baba Vanga never wrote any books, but many books have been written about her, her abilities, and her prophesies. She claimed to receive information from invisible beings and said that, if someone stood before her, she could see the person's life as if it were a movie, from beginning to end. Baba Vanga asked visitors to give her a sugar cube, which she then used as a crystal to focus energy and receive information.

During World War II, crowds flocked to her, hoping that she could reveal clairvoyantly how loved ones in the armed forces were faring or where bodies could be found. On April 8, 1942, Bulgarian King Boris III came to consult with her. Later, during the Communist era, members of the ruling elite sought her advice. It was rumored that Soviet leader Leonid Brezhnev consulted her at least once.

Communist governments, as a rule, persecute or at least do not encourage fortune-tellers, who are considered to be examples or vestiges of primitive superstition. Baba Vanga has been described as the only state-sponsored oracle in modern times. She was studied and analyzed. Allegedly, she had a greater-than-80-percent success rate for locating missing persons. Not all of her predictions were accurate, however. Some did not prove true, or have yet to be proven. (She predicted that World War III would begin in 2010.) Nonetheless, her success rate is impressive.

Vanga foretold Stalin's death; the dissolution of the Soviet Union (a dangerous prediction in Bulgaria at that time and one that could have gotten her into deep political trouble); the September 11 attacks on the United States; the political victory of Boris Yeltsin; the meltdown of the nuclear reactor at Chernobyl; the sinking of the Russian submarine *Kursk* in 2000; and the 2005 victory of Bulgarian grandmaster Veselin Topalov in the world chess tournament. She also predicted an earthquake that hit northern Bulgaria in 1985.

On a personal, rather than political, level, Baba Vanga prophesied the future destinies of babies and children. (She claimed she could see fate, but was powerless to change it.) She claimed to see and converse with people who had died centuries before. She said aliens had been living on Earth among people for centuries, but that, within 200 years, definitive contact would be made.

She was ambivalent about revealing the future. Some accuse her of intentionally failing to deliver bad news. She claimed that she was not permitted to reveal everything she knew to everyone. She allegedly attempted to warn a Bulgarian opera singer not to fly during a certain time. The singer ignored her advice and died in a plane crash.

Baba Vanga used donations given to her by pilgrims and devotees to fund an Orthodox church built according to her specifications. Those specifications were unconventional, and Orthodox bishops initially refused to consecrate the structure. They reconsidered, however, either unwilling to make an enemy of Vanga or of her powerful political patrons. The church has no dome, altar, or alcove for praying, as is customary in Orthodox plans. Its sole ornamentation is portraits of saints painted by Svetlin Roussev, a Bulgarian artist renowned for his experimental art.

Baba Vanga died of complications from breast cancer on August 11, 1996 at age eighty-five. Her will granted all her possessions to the state, including her home, which she hoped would be turned into a museum. The Baba Vanga Museum at 10 Vanga Street in Petrich, Bulgaria opened in 2008 and houses approximately 3,000 items that once belonged to Baba Vanga.

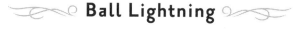

Ball Lightning

Ball lightning is a controversial, usually spherical, flash of light. Like standard lightning, ball lightning may be associated with thunderstorms, but it has also been reported during calm weather. There are many contradictory descriptions of the phenomenon, and it is not certain that all descriptions refer to the same thing. The most basic suggests that ball lightning resembles a luminous ball of lightning or fire that flies through the air with an unpredictable trajectory and ranges in size from as tiny as a pea to several feet in diameter.

In what is now known as the Great Thunderstorm of Widecomb-in-the-Moor, Dartmoor, England, on

Sunday, October 21, 1638, the Church of St. Pancras was struck during an afternoon service by what may have been ball lightning. An eight-inch "ball of fire" struck and entered the building, smashing windows and pews. Stones from the church walls were propelled through wooden beams. The church filled with dark, thick, sulfurous-smelling smoke. The ball of fire divided in two, one half exiting the building by smashing through a window and the other just vanishing within the building. At the time, this celestial ball of fire was interpreted as hellfire or the flaming wrath of God. Four people were killed, approximately sixty were injured, and the building was severely damaged.

Celestial balls of fire have been witnessed over the centuries. They linger and travel—as opposed to lightning, which flashes quickly and then disappears. Ball lightning has occasionally hit ships. In French Caribbean lore, ball lightning is really the dreaded *loup-garou* out on the prowl. A loup-garou is described as a flying werewolf, but is actually a sorcerer who possesses the power to transform into different shapes, including flying animals or a flaming ball of lightning.

Nicholas II, the last tsar of Russia, claimed to see what he called a "fiery ball" while with his grandfather,

Tsar Alexander II, during an all-night vigil in a little church. During a thunderstorm, he observed many flashes of regular lightning and then a fiery ball that flew in the window, whirled around the floor, and exited through the door. On April 30, 1877, a ball of lightning flew into the Golden Temple at Amritsar, India, the holiest of all Sikh shrines, and exited through a side door.

For years, many scientists assumed that reports of ball lightning were either deliberately fraudulent or derived from folklore. Some scientists have proposed that ball lightning may be a form of mass hallucination. Recently, however, the phenomenon has been taken more seriously. One theory suggests that some examples of ball lightning are primordial black holes passing through the Earth's atmosphere. (Scientists hypothesize that primordial black holes were caused by the extreme density of matter during the early expansion of the universe.) Laboratory experiments have produced results that resemble ball lightning, but whether or not these are genuine reproductions is impossible to tell.

Bangs Sisters

Lizzie and May Bangs are considered the foremost practitioners of precipitated spirit paintings. The Bangs sisters served as mediums for spirits who created portraits of the deceased to comfort the living. Although most famous for their precipitated spirit paintings, they were gifted at many forms of mediumship.

Many are convinced that the Bangs sisters were charlatans because their feats defy what seems to be humanly possible. The sisters were under constant observation and investigation, however. Their spirit portraits were created in broad daylight, not in dimly lit rooms. Modern debunkers sometimes presume that earlier generations were just gullible, but, in fact, the Bangs sisters, like other physical mediums, were consistently and frequently challenged by skeptics who sought strenuously to discover how their tricks were accomplished. No evidence of fraud was ever found, however, no matter how closely experts searched.

The Bangs sisters were the daughters of Edward Bangs, a Kansas tinsmith, and Meroe Bangs, also a medium. May Eunice Bangs was born in 1853; Elizabeth Snow Bangs, known as Lizzie, was born in 1859. The family moved to Chicago in 1861 where, from their earliest childhood, the girls assisted their mother with séances. They began their mediumship while still children, producing phenomena such as apports, slate writings, and table tipping. May Bangs was able to manifest a "spirit kitten"—a hairless cat allegedly born on the astral plane. They created a sensation when they produced phenomena while bound within a spirit cabinet. By 1872, May and Lizzie were the stars of the Bangs family séances. By 1888, they were prominent Chicago mediums, and now their mother assisted *them*. The Bangs home was among the leading Spiritualist establishments in Chicago.

The sisters began producing spirit portraits in 1894, serving as mediums for the spirits of Rembrandt and Raphael, who allegedly created their paintings. Art experts who meticulously examined their paintings could not determine the artistic medium that was used. It was not ink, paint, pastel, or any other known substance. Their paintings possess a fine, powdery consistency usually described as similar to the powder found on butterfly wings. They resemble most closely work done with a modern airbrush, a technique that did not exist when the Bangs sisters were alive. Their portraits sold for between $15 and $150—substantial sums of money at that time.

For almost thirty years, the sisters made their summer residence the Spiritualist community of Lily Dale. There, they produced up to three precipitated portraits a day. Their paintings are on display at Lily Dale's Maplewood Hotel, the Lily Dale Museum, Camp Chesterfield, Harmony Grove in Escondido,

California, and elsewhere. The Bangs sisters were prolific, and it is likely that many paintings remain in private collections.

Lizzie passed away on February 22, 1922. No exact date has yet been determined for the death of May Bangs. Census records indicate that, in 1920, she was living in Chicago. Photographs of both sisters appear on a memorial page in the 1922 National Spiritualist Convention souvenir book.

 Boas, Antonio Villas

When Antonio Villas Boas was a twenty-three-year-old farmer in São Francisco de Sales in the Brazilian state of Minas Gerais, he was abducted by aliens—or so he claimed all his life, insisting on the truth of his story until the day he died in 1992. His adventure began on October 16, 1958 when, plowing fields at night to avoid working in the intense daytime heat, he saw what he first thought was a red star that began to descend into his field. As it approached, he saw what he described as an elongated egg-shaped aircraft with a red light in front and what looked like a rotating

cupola on top. Extending three legs, it landed.

Boas tried to escape in his tractor, but the engine failed. He then attempted to flee on foot, but was apprehended by an approximately five-foot-tall being with small blue eyes wearing a gray helmet and what Boas described as a soft, gray unevenly striped siren suit (a one-piece long-sleeved garment similar to a coverall, originally intended for use as an air-raid shelter garment). Three similar beings approached and, together, overpowered Boas and took him to their spacecraft, where he was stripped and covered in some sort of gel. The beings took blood samples from his head and then left him alone for approximately thirty minutes, during which time a yellow gas was pumped into the room that caused him to become nauseous and vomit.

Eventually, a naked female whom he perceived as beautiful entered the room. She had very fair blonde hair, almost platinum, as if bleached with peroxide. Her armpit hair, however, was vividly red, almost the color of blood. Light-skinned with a narrow waist, she had large, well-defined breasts, ample thighs, and small hands and feet. She engaged him in sex, which he found generally pleasurable except for the growling, animal-like sounds she made, which he found disconcerting. When sex was complete, she left. Before she did, however, she pointed at her belly and then up at the sky. Some have interpreted this to mean that she would bear a child, but not on Earth. Other interpretations have also been given.

Boas was brought to another room and permitted to dress. Here, he observed aliens engaged in discussion. He tried to take what looked like a clock as proof of his experiences, but the aliens took it from him before allowing him to exit the craft. He watched as the ship flew off and then went home, where he discovered that approximately four hours had passed. In the following weeks, Boas suffered various physical ailments, including nausea, headaches, and general weakness. Lesions accompanied by light bruises appeared on his skin.

Camp Chesterfield

Now home of the Indiana Association of Spiritualists, Camp Chesterfield was founded in 1886 as a Spiritualist church. It remains a vital, thriving Spiritualist community that offers classes, workshops, seminars, and services year round. Two hotels serve the community. There is also a chapel and a cathedral built in 1954 to replace Camp Chesterfield's original wooden auditorium. The complex also contains a labyrinth. The mission statement of the nearby Hett Art Gallery and Museum is the preservation and display of art and artifacts of the Modern Spiritualist Movement. The museum contains a collection of artifacts associated with the Fox sisters, as well as precipitated spirit portraits by the Bangs sisters. For more information, go to *www.campchesterfield.net*.

Campbell
Brothers

Alongside their fellow Spiritualist mediums, the Bangs sisters, the Campbell brothers are the most renowned creators of precipitated spirit paintings. Like the Bangs, no evidence of fraud was ever discovered in the creation of their pieces, no matter how closely they were examined or investigated. Unlike the Bangs sisters, however, the Campbell brothers were not actually siblings. Instead, they have been described as "boon companions." During their era, the safest way for gay men to travel together, maintaining their relationship as well as their privacy, was to profess to be brothers.

Born in England in 1833, Allen Campbell immigrated to the United States, where he eventually ran an import-export business in Atlantic City, New Jersey. Little else is known of his private life. Nor is any birth date presently known for Charles Shourds, also known as Charles Campbell.

The first documented reference to the Campbell brothers as a mediumship team occurs in 1892. Among other feats of physical mediumship, they created precipitated spirit portraits on canvas and porcelain. They produced portraits for individuals seeking images of loved ones, as well as portraits of well-known figures, including Otto Von Bismarck, Napoleon Bonaparte, and, most famously, Abraham Lincoln.

Allen died in an Atlantic City hospital in 1919; Charles died in Lily Dale on August 23, 1926. Following Charles' death, their combined ashes were cast into the Atlantic Ocean off the shores of Atlantic City. Their work is on display in Lily Dale.

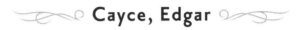

Cayce, Edgar

Edgar Cayce (pronounced *Casey*) was born on a farm near Hopkinsville, Kentucky on March 18, 1877. He is known as the "sleeping prophet" because he delivered his prophesies while in a trance state resembling sleep. He gave over 14,000 readings to thousands of people over a period of forty-three years, accurately diagnosing illness and recommending treatments that proved to be effective.

Cayce's psychic gifts manifested early. When he was six, he told his parents that he could see visions and converse with dead relatives. His parents didn't believe him. They could see, however, that Cayce could memorize pages of a book merely by placing it beneath  his pillow and sleeping on it. When he awoke, he could quote lengthy passages verbatim. At age thirteen, Cayce had a vision of a goddess-like being who asked what he most desired. He told her he wished to help others, especially sick children.

In 1899, Cayce—then twenty-two, not particularly well-educated, and working as a salesman—suffered paralysis of the throat, something like severe laryngitis, which prevented him from speaking. Physicians were unable to heal him, although he consulted many. This lasted for months. Unable to work in sales, he became a photographer's assistant because it was a job where he wouldn't have to speak.

A traveling entertainer hypnotized Cayce and discovered that, under hypnosis, Cayce's voice returned. As soon as he was out of the trance, however, his condition returned. Puzzled, Cayce consulted a local hypnotist, Al Layne, on March 31, 1901. In a hypnotic trance, Cayce, questioned by Layne, was able to determine his own effective treatment, and his voice was immediately restored. Layne himself suffered from a chronic stomach ailment that physicians had been unable to relieve. He asked Cayce to enter a trance and recommend a cure for him. Although reluctant, Cayce agreed. Entranced, he recommended a series of exercises and dietary changes. Within a week, Layne was cured.

Word spread about Cayce's abilities and people flocked to him, seeking healing. Although he wished to pursue photography, Cayce was unable to refuse those seeking help. In his trance state, Cayce displayed medical knowledge that he did not consciously possess. His ability to provide "trance diagnoses" brought him celebrity. After the *New York Times* featured an article about him with the headline, "Illiterate

Man Becomes Doctor When Hypnotized," he was swamped with pleas for help.

When visitors arrived for consultations, Cayce hypnotized himself by lying down on a sofa, folding his hands over his stomach, closing his eyes, and falling into a sleep-like trance. These entranced consultations became known as his "readings." In this meditative state, he claimed he was able to access the Akashic Records, through which he was able to answer questions both historical ("How were the pyramids built?") and personal ("Why does my hip hurt?"). Eventually, Cayce was able to diagnose without a client's physical presence. A name and address were sufficient for him to provide information.

While entranced, Cayce also discussed metaphysical and mystical topics like astrology, with which he was completely unfamiliar in waking life. In 1923, while in a trance, he was asked about life after death. His own response, which he learned only upon awakening, shocked him. He discovered that he had been discussing reincarnation, a doctrine in which, as a devout Christian, he himself did not believe, although he eventually came to accept that whatever he had said in trance was true. Cayce, a church-going, Sunday-school-teaching member of the Disciples of Christ, discussed reincarnation in nearly 2,000 readings.

Entranced, Cayce offered detailed descriptions of Atlantis. He described Jesus as a member of a Jewish sect, the Essenes, who had traveled to India in his youth to study Eastern spirituality. Cayce encouraged everyone to record their own dreams and have them interpreted. He suggested that becoming more spiritual was the key to becoming more psychic.

Cayce predicted the beginnings and ends of both world wars, as well as the possibility of a third one. In 1939, he foretold the deaths of two presidents while they were still in office. These are now interpreted as being Franklin D. Roosevelt, who died in office in 1945, and John F. Kennedy, assassinated in 1963.

In 1931, Cayce founded the Association for Research and Enlightenment (ARE) with the goal of furthering research into holistic health, personal spirituality, and ancient mysteries. Cayce did not directly ask clients for money. Instead, people seeking readings were asked to join the ARE, thus protecting Cayce from charges of fortune-telling, which was illegal in many states.

Edgar Cayce died on January 3, 1945, but ARE survives him. Its mission is to help people improve their lives through information given by Edgar Cayce. Over 14,000 case histories of his readings are available for reference at ARE. Its headquarters in Virginia Beach includes a stone labyrinth, a meditation center, a health center, and a day spa. ARE runs Cayce study groups, and there are Edgar Cayce Centers in thirty-seven nations. For more information, go to *www.edgarcayce.org*.

Channeling

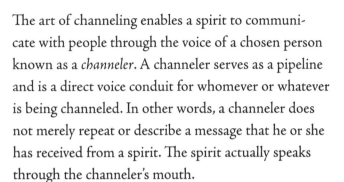

The art of channeling enables a spirit to communicate with people through the voice of a chosen person known as a *channeler*. A channeler serves as a pipeline and is a direct voice conduit for whomever or whatever is being channeled. In other words, a channeler does not merely repeat or describe a message that he or she has received from a spirit. The spirit actually speaks through the channeler's mouth.

A channeler's voice may or may not change. Channelers may reveal knowledge that they do not consciously possess or speak in languages that they do not consciously know. While entranced, medium Laura Edmonds, daughter of New York State Supreme Court Judge John Worth Edmonds, was able to speak nine different languages, including French, Greek, Hungarian, Latin, and Portuguese, although consciously she was able to speak only English and a smidgen of French.

A channeler is a type of medium, but not all mediums are channelers. Some channelers engage in automatic writing rather than speaking the words of others, but comparatively few demonstrate other paranormal talents like clairvoyance, clairaudience, or psychometry. Most channelers only channel a single entity, typically beings from other planes of existence with messages for humanity as a whole, rather than for specific people. Channelers tend to deliver lectures or sermons, not private messages.

When a medium delivers a message from someone's dead grandfather that no one else on Earth could have known, it gives a sense of being a genuine and valid experience. It is not always easy, however, to identify channeled beings or prove the validity of their messages. In general, these are not spirits of the dearly departed, nor are they familiar spirits from mythology or from various spiritual traditions. Instead, many are unique spirits who identify themselves as coming from other planets or from lost continents like Atlantis.

Channeling is not a new phenomenon. Ancient prophets, priestesses, and sibyls can all be understood as channelers. The most famous modern channeler was Jane Roberts, who gave voice to the entity known as Seth.

Chupacabra

The *chupacabra*, a cryptid that allegedly inhabits the Americas, is held responsible for numerous vicious livestock killings. Chupacabras are currently believed to range as far south as Chile and as far north as Maine. Since 2006, there have been rumored sightings in Russia as well, accompanied by reported attacks on local animals.

The name chupacabra derives from two Spanish words—*chupar* ("to suck") and *cabra* ("goat"). *Chupacabra* literally means "goat sucker," and that name is meant literally. Chupacabras are vampiric creatures who consume the blood of livestock, especially goats. They do not behave like any known species of vampire bat, which may consume relatively minimal amounts of blood, returning to feed repeatedly. Instead, the chupacabra drains victims and may mangle and eviscerate them. No definitive evidence of the chupacabra has yet been collected, but there are many eyewitness reports.

Chupacabras were first identified in Puerto Rico where, in 1995, eight sheep were discovered completely drained of blood and sporting puncture wounds on their chests. This was followed by further sightings and alleged chupacabra attacks in Puerto Rico, other Caribbean islands, Mexico, and the United States. Some now suspect that chupacabras may be responsible for similar attacks on Puerto Rican livestock dating back to 1975 that had been previously attributed to "Satanic cults." Science currently denies the existence of this creature. But if, as many scientists insist, the chupacabra does not exist, then who or what is responsible for the strange deaths of all these animals?

Descriptions of the chupacabra vary. It has been described as resembling a cross between a reptile and a canine, and some believe it to be just such a hybrid, although scientifically speaking, that should be impossible. It is reportedly about the size of a very large dog with leathery or scaly skin and a row of sharp spines, spikes, or bristles ranging down its back. It may be some sort of unknown wild canine, and it is sometimes described as resembling a hairless coyote or dog. It may have fangs and a forked tongue, and emits a sulfurous stench. When confronted, its eyes are said to glow strangely red. It screeches.

The chupacabra may be a natural, but previously unknown, creature, perhaps once hidden in the jungle but now venturing out because of habitat loss. Some attribute extraterrestrial origins to it. Is the chupacabra an alien pet left behind?

Chupacabras have been reported in many of the same areas as UFO sightings. Some witnesses claim to have seen reptilian aliens departing landed spacecraft with chupacabra-like creatures running at their heels like dogs. Is it possible that an alien craft left chupacabras behind in the same way that humans have been known to abandon pets in the woods or along roads?

Chupacabras have become great media favorites, featured in video games, children's cartoons like *Scooby-Doo*, and television shows like the *X-Files*. Cute chupacabra plush toys are available. There is a brand of Chupacabras Pale Ale and Chupacabra California red wine.

 Clairaudience

Clairaudience literally means "clear hearing." Some describe clairaudience as hearing with the spiritual ear. Think of it as extrasensory perception received as sound. Those gifted with this psychic talent may

hear voices, although the voices will not manifest aloud. Others present will not hear them unless they, too, are clairaudient—and possibly not even then.

Not every clairaudient experiences this paranormal, psychic skill in the same manner. The most common clairaudient experience is hearing your own name called when no one is there or no one has called. Clairaudients may hear anonymous voices or the voices of loved ones. Some may experience clairaudience only under personally stressful conditions—for example, in an emergency they hear their own child calling to them from miles away. Others receive constant prophetic messages and may be able to harness this power to become a professional psychic. Some clairaudients literally hear whispering in their ears, although no other person is present. Another clairaudient skill is the ability to have flashes of psychic insight triggered by voices or music or other sounds. The most famous clairaudient may be Joan of Arc, who led France to victory by obeying voices that only she could hear.

 ## Clairsentience

Clairsentience literally means "clear feeling" and refers to extrasensory perception received as physical sensation. Clairsentience is similar to empathy, but is experienced more profoundly. Many clairsentients are gifted healers: they can feel the pain of others and thus are able to identify, locate, and treat it. They can literally feel the pain of those near them.

Clairsentients may sense more than just aches, pains, and illness. Some feel sensations of heat, cold, or hunger. Some feel emotional pain or, conversely, joy and happiness. Sitting in a room with two other people, a clairsentient can feel the love or enmity they feel for each other. This can be an overwhelming gift.

Clairvoyance

Clairvoyance literally means "clear sight." A clairvoyant is a "clear seer." This ability to see distant, future, or past events is perhaps the most famous form of psychic prowess.

What clairvoyants see varies. Not all clairvoyants possess the same powers or skills. Clairvoyant mediums may be able to see (and describe) spirits who are invisible to others. Some clairvoyants can see events happening in distant locations or in the future or past. Some can read letters within sealed envelopes. Some can put their hands on a book and "see" the words printed within. A classic example of a clairvoyant is the Bible's Witch

of Endor, who summoned and was able to see the spirit of the prophet Samuel when she was asked to do so by King Saul.

Cold Spots

Have you ever been swimming in the ocean and encountered an especially warm spot? Paranormal cold spots are similar, but they occur on land. Cold spots are small areas that feel significantly colder than surrounding areas with no conventionally discernible reason for this localized drop in temperature. In other words, the spot directly in front of an air conditioner does not count as a paranormal cold spot.

Thermometers do not always register cold spots, although sometimes they do. Cold spots may be temporary. They may exist for brief periods, or they may be located consistently in the same place. Some cold spots move. Not everyone can feel the same cold spots. Some people are more sensitive to them than others, and this may be an indication of psychic ability or mediumship potential.

These drops in temperature may indicate the presence of ghosts. Ghost hunters may thus utilize thermal sensors or thermal imaging to locate cold spots. Infrared (IR) thermometers, also known as laser thermometers, can measure temperatures remotely. (Some people feel shivers when ghosts are present rather than a sense that an area is cold.)

Movies and television programs frequently indicate the presence of a ghost by making the breath of living characters visible, demonstrating how chilly an area has suddenly become, for example in M. Night Shyamalan's *The Sixth Sense* and in the television series *Supernatural*.

Contactees

Contactees are people who claim to experience repeated contact with extraterrestrials or who claim to have continuous relationships with them. Not all contactees claim to have had physical contact with aliens, although some do. This contact may be telepathic or through devices like Ouija boards. Some contactees claim to channel information received from extraterrestrial sources. Many develop relationships with extraterrestrials that resemble the relationships others have with spirit guides.

Contactees tend to describe aliens as benevolent beings, as opposed to abductees who report being victimized. Skeptics tend to classify contactees as the lunatic fringe of the UFO community. They are commonly accused of being delusional or hoaxers. Some ufologists suggest that at least some contactees may be government operatives seeking to discredit serious UFO research. Many contactees are spiritually oriented New Agers, which is a source of friction between them and those in the UFO community who are oriented exclusively toward hard science.

George Adamski (1891–1965) is considered the first documented contactee, the first to come forward and tell his story publicly. Adamski claimed to have first witnessed a cigar-shaped spaceship in 1946. Then, on November 20, 1952 at 12:30 in the afternoon, he encountered Orthon, a traveler from the planet Venus, in California's Colorado Desert. Orthon, who had long blonde hair, warned Adamski of the dangers of nuclear war and took him traveling in his spaceship. Adamski published a book about his experiences and became a popular lecturer.

Another famous contactee, Dr. Daniel Fry (1908–1992), was the engineer in charge of installing instruments for missile control and guidance at White Sands Proving Ground when he was taken for a ride in an alien spaceship—or so he describes in his book, *The White Sands Incident* (Horus House Press, 1992). Fry developed a relationship with an alien named A-lan (pronounced *ah-lawhn*), his host on the aircraft, who advised him to inform others of the spiritual benefits of extraterrestrial contact.

Crop Circles

Crop circles are patterns that appear mysteriously in grain fields, formed from selectively flattened cereal crops like wheat, barley, rapeseed, and rye. These geometric patterns, usually but not always circular, are discovered in the morning, apparently created overnight.

Because not all of them are circular, some prefer to call them "crop formations." They are also popularly known as "grain graffiti."

The grain is rarely cut or damaged but is instead pressed down, often with stems uniformly bent in the same direction. Young plants may continue to ripen even after being pushed down. Some crop circles are huge, as large as two football fields. Many are mathematically perfect, demonstrating no geometric errors despite their size and their having been created in darkness. Crop circles are generally best appreciated when viewed from a helicopter or plane.

Crop circles are an international phenomenon, manifesting in over twenty countries including Canada and the United States. In Japan, one was discovered in a rice paddy that simultaneously and mysteriously lost a substantial quantity of water, as if it had been partially drained. The greatest concentration of crop circles, however, is in southern England, which is also where they were first perceived as paranormal phenomena worthy of media attention.

Crop circles first came to international attention during the 1970s. By the 1980s, they were a media sensation. The crop circles of the 1970s and 1980s were simple circular forms. In 1990, however, linear patterns began to emerge, including some comprised of straight lines. Crop circles evolved into complex geometric and fractal formations that incorporate spirals as well as shamanic and alchemical symbols. Some crop circles resemble mazes and labyrinths; one formation appeared to depict a gigantic jellyfish.

Although not widely documented before the 1970s, some evidence indicates that crop circles are not a new phenomenon—most notably a woodcut featured on the cover of an English pamphlet entitled "The Mowing Devil or Strange News out of Hartfordshire" published in 1678. This pamphlet recounts the saga of a farmer who, offended by the price a laborer demanded to mow his field, swore that he'd rather pay the devil to do it instead. That night, the farmer's field appeared to be on fire. In the morning, however, no evidence of burning was evident. Instead, the field was mowed, albeit too perfectly to have been accomplished by human hands. The woodcut depicts a devil creating what is clearly a crop circle.

Crop circles seem to possess an affinity for sacred sites, appearing with regularity and in great concentration near the ancient stone circles at Avebury and

Stonehenge in England, as well as near Silbury Hill, Europe's largest Neolithic mound. In the United States, a crop circle was discovered near the Great Serpent Mound. Crop circles often also appear in areas associated with UFO sightings.

Many crop circles manifest electromagnetic anomalies, leading to speculation that they project some sort of electromagnetic field. There are reports of cell phones and electronic equipment malfunctioning when carried within some circles. These devices then mysteriously recover mere inches beyond the perimeter of the circle. Likewise, some describe batteries that inexplicably drain within a circle, only to work perfectly once brought outside. Some people claim to experience tingling sensations when they walk within the circles. The circles of greatest interest to paranormal researchers are those displaying these sorts of anomalies, especially if they are also mathematically perfect.

In the summer of 1991, Doug Bower and Dave Chorley, two men from Southampton, England, claimed that, beginning in 1978, they created a number of crop circles as a prank. Their first attempt, they said, was forty feet in diameter and took fifteen minutes to construct using planks, rope, wire, and hats. In response, many debunkers were quick to dismiss all crop circles as hoaxes. Doug and Dave's confessions contained numerous discrepancies, however, and some conspiracy theorists suggest that they were staged by the US Air Force, the CIA, the British Ministry of

Defense, the Royal Air Force, or some or all of these organizations acting in collusion in an attempt to deflect attention from the true origin of crop circles.

Some crop circles are now openly and proudly created by human hands. Many are exceptionally beautiful and are described as a kind of "Earth art." Since the early 1990s, Circlemakers, a UK arts collective, has crafted circles for artistic expression as well as for commercial use. In July 1992, a crop-circle-making competition was held in England. A growing subculture of crop-circle enthusiasts exists whose members are known as "croppies."

The origins of other circles remain mysterious and continue to stymie investigators. Experiments indicate that some kind of microwave energy may be responsible for or somehow involved in the creation of crop circles. Many theories exist, but none yet explain conclusively how these circles are formed. Extraterrestrials are credited with creating some as messages for humanity. Crop circles may also be a natural by-product of powerful terrestrial energies and may indicate some sort of natural energy source, similar to ley lines or telluric currents.

 **Cryptids**

Is it reasonable to believe that we have catalogued all the creatures who share our planet? Perhaps not. After all, the gorilla remained undiscovered by

Western science until the early 19th century, before which reports of this giant ape were routinely dismissed as fanciful.

Likewise, cryptids are living beings whose existence is not acknowledged or verified by science. The study of cryptids is known as cryptozoology. Science does not officially acknowledge the existence of cryptids because there is no definitive proof that they exist. Individual creatures, living or dead, are unavailable for examination. Photographic evidence is inconclusive. The evidence that does exist—footprints, for example—is considered insufficient for proof. That said, many individuals claim to have sighted or encountered these creatures.

Cryptids include dragons, phoenixes, and unicorns that have been the stuff of legend and lore for centuries, as well as creatures that individuals claim to have sighted but for which there is no proof—or, at least, not yet. An extremely lengthy list of these creatures exists. Some of the most famous, like the yeti and chupacabra, are described in this book. A much more extensive exploration of them can be found in its companion volume, *The Weiser Field Guide to Cryptozoology*.

◦ Crystal Skull ◦

Superficially, the topic of crystal skulls seems straightforward. Crystal skulls are detailed replicas of human skulls carved from quartz crystal. That description, however, is the only straightforward thing about them. Crystal skulls are the subject of much fascination and heated debate because of the many mysteries surrounding them.

- Who carved these skulls?
- How old are they?
- What was their original purpose?
- How were they carved?
- Do these skulls possess paranormal powers?

With the exception of the last one, these questions may seem academic, but they are not. Although we can date the crystal from which these skulls are carved, precisely *when* they were carved remains a mystery. Nor in many cases can we determine conclusively what types of tools were used.

Most crystal skulls are generally believed to be Mesoamerican—either Aztec or Mayan—and to date from pre-Columbian times, meaning that they were carved before Columbus and other Europeans arrived in the Americas. (There are also Peruvian crystal skulls and Chinese jade skulls that are believed to possess paranormal powers.) This remains unverified and experts who have examined some skulls suggest that they were carved in Europe in the mid 19th century.

One thing is sure, however. These skulls were not created by primitive carving tools. Increasingly sophisticated testing methods suggest that at least some were created using modern technology, leading to yet another mystery. Who had access to this technology so long before the testing existed to identify it?

Part of the mystery is that, regardless of how ancient they may be, crystal skulls were unknown before the 19th and 20th centuries. If they existed before that, then they were carefully protected mystic secrets. The provenance of most crystal skulls is murky. They do not figure in surviving Mesoamerican myth or folklore, but the key word there is *surviving*. Vast quantities of information and artifacts were destroyed following the advent of the conquistadors and Christianity, and huge historical gaps now exist. Was information about crystal skulls destroyed? We may never know. Skulls certainly do play a significant role

in traditional Central and South American spirituality, with vestiges preserved in modern Mexican Day of the Dead paraphernalia like sugar skulls and life-size papier mâché skulls.

Many of the earliest crystal skulls brought to public attention arrived courtesy of French antiquarian and archaeologist Eugène Boban (1834–1908). Boban, an expert on Mexican art, spent much of his life in Mexico and spoke fluent Spanish and Nahuatl, the language of the Aztecs. Did he find his skulls in Mexico as he claimed, or did he secretly commission European carvers to create them so that he could sell them as rare and expensive Mexican antiques?

Other more exotic origins for crystal skulls have also been suggested—for example, that they were rescued from Atlantis prior to its destruction or that they are extraterrestrial in origin, meaning that, regardless of where they were found on Earth, they originally came from outer space.

Crystal skulls range in size from as small as a bead to a few inches to life-size to larger-than-life, but fascination tends to be with those that are at least life-size. Quartz is a key component in many modern technologies, including computers and telecommunication devices. Quartz makes it possible to program a computer, store memory, and retrieve information. A miniscule quartz chip holds massive quantities of information, including thousands of images, songs, photographs, videos, and other data. What then is the information-storing capacity of a life-size quartz-crystal skull? Were ancient people aware of the information-storage capacity of crystal? Did they create crystal skulls to store, record, and transmit data?

According to one legend, thirteen crystal skulls were distributed throughout what is now Latin America. (Numbers vary, with different versions of the legend suggesting more than fifty skulls.) The skulls are purportedly the equivalent of a multivolume encyclopedia, each one a separate book. At a pivotal moment, the skulls will be reunited so that they can reactivate the knowledge they contain and guide a new age. Some believe that this pivotal moment will be in 2012.

Regardless of origin or initial purpose, crystal skulls have developed modern New Age and occult uses. They serve as divination tools, similar to traditional crystal balls. Some crystal skulls are believed to have the power to enhance or activate human psychic abilities. They are considered receivers and transmitters of energy. Some crystal skulls allegedly possess healing properties, including the power to heal serious diseases like cancer. Even modern crystal skulls may manifest these powers. Contemporary skulls are allegedly activated by bringing them to sacred places or into contact with other skulls, especially ancient ones.

Several crystal skulls are owned by the Smithsonian Museum, the British Museum, and the Musée de Quai Branly in Paris. Crystal skulls are featured in the 2008 movie *Indiana Jones and the Kingdom of the Crystal Skull*, which is based on the legend of the thirteen skulls, as well as in many other movies, novels, and video games.

Crystal Skull of Doom

The most famous crystal skull is the so-called Lubaantun Skull, also known as the Mitchell-Hedges Skull and, most sensationally, as the Crystal Skull of

Doom. An 11.91-pound, highly polished crystal skull the size of a small human cranium, it exhibits the highest quality of all known, allegedly Central American, crystal skulls. Unlike some other crystal skulls, this one has a detachable jaw.

The Skull of Doom's age is unknown, as is its origin. Arguments suggest that it is Mayan, Aztec, or something else now unknown, possibly extraterrestrial. The crystal from which it is carved is similar to crystal quarried in California, but scientists have been unable to determine its origin conclusively. It is unclear what tools were used to carve it. Art restorer Frank Dorland, who studied the skull for six years, claimed he could not see typical carving or scratch marks. He theorized that the skull was cut with diamond tools and then polished with sand over a lengthy period. Further tests showed traces of metallic grinding on the detachable jaw's teeth.

The Crystal Skull of Doom was first brought to public attention in the 1950s by Frederick Mitchell-Hedges (1882–1959), the archaeologist, explorer, and radio host rumored to be the inspiration for the fictional character Indiana Jones. He claimed that his adopted daughter, Anna Mitchell-Hedges, found it on January 1, 1924, her seventeenth birthday, beneath an altar amid the ruins of an ancient Mayan city, Lubaantun, now in Belize, but then in British Honduras.

According to Mitchell-Hedges, local Mayans told him the skull had been used by Mayan high priests as a cursing device, a tool intended to focus killing energy. Skeptics claim that Mitchell-Hedges fabricated a romantic story and that records indicate that he really purchased the skull in England in the 1940s. Some suggest that he brought the skull to Belize, planting it in the ruins so that Anna would have the pleasure of "discovering" it.

Mitchell-Hedges' account does contain discrepancies. The skull does not appear among his writings from Lubaantun, although one would assume that such a sensational discovery would be mentioned. Other participants at the archaeological dig claim not to recall either the discovery or Anna's presence.

To her dying day, Anna insisted that she had found the skull and said that the reason it was not written up in field notes was that, if the skull's discovery were publicized, Mitchell-Hedges would have been obligated to turn it over to a museum and that he wanted to let local Mayans keep it. Anna said that, when her family was preparing to leave Lubaantun, the Mayans to whom the skull had been entrusted gave it to Mitchell-Hedges as a gift. He brought it to England where, later, in financial straits, he used it as collateral. When Mitchell-Hedges purchased the skull in the 1940s, according to Anna, he was only buying back his own property.

Mitchell-Hedges briefly mentioned the crystal skull in the first edition of his 1954 autobiography, *Danger My Ally*, but did not discuss where it was found or by whom. All mention of the skull was omitted from later editions. Before his death, Mitchell-Hedges left a cryptic message regarding the skull: "How it came into my possession I have reason for not revealing." Upon his death, Anna inherited the skull.

The Crystal Skull of Doom reputedly possesses paranormal powers. It can allegedly induce trance states in those who gaze within it, contemplate it, or are even just in close proximity to it. Allegedly, some have gone insane in its presence, with the implication that the skull is to blame. Some claim the skull emits fragrant perfume and mysterious sounds. Images of mountains and temples allegedly appear within it.

From 1967 until her death in 2007, Anna Mitchell-Hedges took her crystal skull on tour, allowing people contact with it on a pay-per-view basis. This gave them more contact than they would have been allowed had the skull been in a museum. Upon her death, her friend Bill Homann became the skull's caretaker. He renamed it the Crystal Skull of Love, emphasizing his belief that its true purpose is to assist humanity. For more information, go to *www.mitchell-hedges.com*.

Dogon

The Dogon are an ethnic group living in Mali, approximately 300 miles south of Timbuktu in West Africa. They claim to possess information received from visitors from Sirius, a star that is 8.7 light-years from Earth. Sirius, the brightest star in the night sky, is also known as the Dog Star.

The Dogon claim that Sirius has a dense and extremely heavy dark companion that is invisible to the naked eye. In fact, this is correct: Sirius does have a dark companion, now called Sirius B. The existence of Sirius B, first suspected by Western astronomers in the mid 19th century, was first observed in 1862, but not described in detail until the 1920s. It was only in 1928 that British astrophysicist Sir Arthur Eddington proposed the theory of white dwarfs—stars whose atoms have collapsed inward so that a pea-sized piece may weigh half a ton. Sirius B is roughly the size of Earth, but weighs as much as our Sun. It moves in an elliptical fifty-year orbit.

Dogon stargazing was first revealed to the West by two French anthropologists, Marcel Griaule and Germaine Dieterlen, in a paper entitled "A Sudanese Sirius System," published in 1950 in the *Journal de la Société des Africainistes*. (*Sudanese* was once used to indicate all of sub-Saharan Africa, not just the modern nation of Sudan.) Griaule and Dieterlen had lived among the Dogon since 1931. In 1946, Griaule was initiated into a Dogon religious society and so became privy to spiritual secrets.

According to Dogon lore, extraterrestrial fish-like creatures called the *Nommo* traveled to Earth for the purpose of civilizing humanity. They arrived in an ark, which landed to the northwest of present Dogon territory, the region from which the Dogon originate. Their description of the ark has led many to associate it with alien spacecraft. The ark created a dust storm as it skidded to a landing. A visible flame was extinguished after the ark touched ground.

The Dogon say that the Nommo came from a celestial body that, like Sirius B, rotates around Sirius, but whose weight is only a quarter of Sirius B's. To date, this planet, dubbed Sirius C, remains undiscovered. Sirius is 3.5 times as hot and bright as our Sun, so scientists theorize that any planet in its solar system must be in its far reaches in order for life to survive there. This would almost certainly make it invisible to current telescopes. In fact, the only reason that Sirius B was discovered was because its weight affects the orbit of Sirius itself.

When Griaule arrived, the Dogon were an extremely isolated people, living in villages built along a sandstone escarpment in Mali's central plateau. They had chosen to live in this tremendously remote locale in the 15th century in an attempt to avoid forced Islamic conversions and also to prevent their being sold into slavery as punishment for refusing to convert.

The Dogon possessed extraordinarily detailed, sophisticated, and accurate knowledge of the solar system. They knew that the planets revolved around the Sun. They described the terrain of the Moon as "dry and dead." They were aware of Jupiter's moons, first seen in the West through a telescope by Galileo. The Dogon drew pictures of Saturn with a ring around it, also only visible through a telescope. When the Dogon drew the elliptical orbit of Sirius B, they showed the star off-center, not in the orbit's center.

How did these isolated people who lacked astronomical equipment gain planetary information that is invisible to the unassisted human eye? How were people who resided in the middle of nowhere and lacked what the West considers education and technology able to discuss sophisticated concepts like planetary weight? The Dogon lacked even rudimentary telescopes. How did they do it?

There are at least three different theories of how the Dogon acquired their knowledge. First, we can take the Dogon at their word. Perhaps they did learn celestial secrets from benevolent aliens. Second, skeptics suggest that Griaule and Dieterlen, who went to live among the Dogon three years after Eddington first postulated his theory of white dwarfs, may have brought this theory with them, inspiring the Dogon tale. A third theory suggests that the ancestors of the Dogon may be refugees from ancient Egypt or had early contact with Egyptians.

Sirius was the most important star in ancient Egyptian cosmology. Associated with the deity Anubis, canine lord of the dead, the rising of Sirius signalled the annual return of the Nile floods, upon which Egyptian civilization depended. Although nothing reminiscent of the Nommo appears in surviving Egyptian mythology, this may have been information revealed only to initiates. It was not common knowledge in Dogon society before the anthropologists published their paper, which received tremendous worldwide attention. Griaule did not know of the Nommo prior to his own initiation into a secret religious society.

Sirius is associated with the rising waters of Earth's longest river. Moreover, given what we know, any planet in the Sirius system that could potentially support life would be hot and steamy, and its inhabitants would likely be comprised of amphibious creatures that require proximity to water. The Nommo are said to be amphibious. This Dogon legend is reminiscent of ancient Babylonian mythology and the Lovecraftian mythos.

Doyle, Sir Arthur Conan

Most famous as the creator of Sherlock Holmes, Arthur Ignatius Doyle was born on May 22, 1859 in Edinburgh, Scotland to an artistic Irish Catholic family. (He later added "Conan" to his surname himself.) His father, Charles Altamont Doyle (1832–1893), was an artist who specialized in fairy-themed paintings. His mother, Mary Foley, was a brilliant storyteller.

When he was nine, wealthy members of the Doyle family offered to pay for Arthur's education. He was sent to a Jesuit boarding school in England for seven years, which he loathed but where he discovered his talent for storytelling. Following graduation, Doyle pursued a career in medicine, studying at the University of Edinburgh. He opened a practice in Portsmouth, married in 1885, and by March 1886 was hard at work writing *A Study in Scarlet*, the novel that changed his life. *A Study in Scarlet* introduced the characters Sherlock Holmes and his compatriot Dr. Watson, making Doyle an international celebrity.

Doyle was ambivalent about Holmes, his most famous creation, killing the character off at one point, although he eventually resurrected him in response to public demand as well as his own personal financial demands. Doyle, a prolific writer who authored many other works, always sought to be appreciated as a serious, philosophical artist rather than just a popular author.

The death of his father, whom Arthur had been forced to commit to an institution for depression and alcoholism, troubled him deeply. Three weeks later, in 1893, Arthur joined the Society for Psychical Research

(SPR) and began his evolution into a very public Spiritualist and paranormal investigator.

Readers identified Doyle with his character Holmes and held him up as a paragon of what was considered to be "rational thought." Many were very disturbed by Doyle's deep fascination with and commitment to Spiritualism. Doyle became controversial and was often subject to ridicule and mockery.

Doyle authored several Spiritualist works, including *The History of Spiritualism* published at his own expense in 1924, as well as *The Case for Spirit Photography* and *Wanderings of a Spiritualist*. His Spiritualist novel, *The Land of Mist*, was published in 1924. Another novel, *The Mystery of Cloomber*, is a supernatural mystery involving Buddhist monks who mete out justice in the afterlife. He also operated a Spiritualist bookstore. In 1925, Doyle was elected honorary president of the International Spiritualist Congress in Paris. He died on July 7, 1930.

Dropa

Did aliens crash-land their aircraft 12,000 years ago in the remote mountains near the Tibetan border in China's Qinhai Province?

In 1937 and 1938, an expedition led by Chi Pu Tei, professor of archaeology at Beijing University, was exploring a series of caves in the remote Himalayas when they discovered neatly arranged rows of tombs containing 4-foot-4-inch skeletons with abnormally large heads, long arms, and thin fragile bodies. The identity of the small bodies was puzzling. Someone suggested that they might be a species of previously unknown mountain gorillas. Professor Chi Pu Tei's succinct response was: "Who ever heard of apes burying each other?"

The caves in which the tombs were found, sometimes called China's Roswell, had been artificially expanded and carved into a series of tunnels and subterranean storerooms. The walls were squared and glazed using an unknown, but massive, heat-producing process. Pictures of the Moon, the stars, and the rising Sun, a mountainous landscape, and lines of dots connecting the Earth with the sky were carved into the cave walls. Nothing that was recognizably an epitaph was discovered near the graves, but hundreds of one-foot-wide stone discs with ¾-inch-wide holes in their centers were found. These discs, allegedly inscribed with spiraling grooves from the edge to the center hole, are now known as Dropa stones, also spelled Drokpa or Dzopa, the Tibetan spelling. The aliens alleged to have created them are called the Dropa.

The Dropa stones were labeled, removed, and placed in storage in Beijing University for twenty years, along with other expedition artifacts. Attempts to decipher them were unsuccessful. Then, in 1958, Professor Tsum Um Nui was allowed to examine the discs. He concluded that what appeared to be grooves were really tiny hieroglyphs, many of which had eroded away. Dr. Tsum claimed to have deciphered the hieroglyphs and said they described the crash landing of the Dropa spaceship. The majority of the crash survivors had been attacked and killed by local people. The discs expressed regret that the crash had occurred in such a remote locale, because it made repairing their craft or building a new one impossible. The Dropa were trapped, unable to return to their home planet.

In fact, local legends from the region where the discs and skeletons were found describe small, big-headed people with puny little legs who fell from the clouds. Because they were perceived as strange and ugly—and because they fell from the sky—local people feared them and hunted them down, although eventually peace and coexistence were established.

Professor Tsum published his findings in a professional journal in 1962, but he was severely mocked, which the Chinese government found humiliating. Tsum was never again permitted to publish or even discuss his findings. He fled China during the Cultural Revolution and died in Japan in the 1960s. (It is suggested, based on his name, that Tsum was of Japanese ancestry.) In 1965, Professor Chi Pu Tei and four colleagues were permitted to discuss their find. Their interpretations of the grooved discs correspond with those of Professor Tsum.

Some discs were sent to Moscow for further examination. There, the Dropa stones and drawings were determined to be approximately 12,000 years old. Chemical analysis indicated substantial quantities of cobalt and other metallic substances. Apparently, Soviet researchers saw a resemblance to phonograph records and allegedly constructed a special turntable for the discs. When placed on the rotating turntable, the discs were said to hum or vibrate rhythmically, as if an electrical charge were passing through them.

Skeptics insist the Dropa are a hoax and that Tsum never existed. Indeed, no evidence of him exists. No explanations have been offered for how the unknown hieroglyphs were translated. Discs allegedly stored in Beijing and Moscow have not been brought forth for corroboration or inspection. However, one could easily argue that important evidence was destroyed during the Chinese Cultural Revolution or remains concealed by the Chinese government. Was Tsum's identity erased?

Photos currently circulating that ostensibly show Dropa discs actually display Bi discs, flat circles carved from jade or nephrite featuring a circle or square in the center, reminiscent of traditional Chinese coins. Thousands of Bi discs have been found in China, mostly in southern regions and often in gravesites. Most are Neolithic (c. 3000 B.C.E.), but some are older. Some are simple; others are ornately carved with dragon, fish, or snake motifs. None have markings similar to the Dropa stones. Some theorize that the Bi discs may be modeled after Dropa discs.

Ectoplasm

Ectoplasm is a mysterious substance associated with ghosts and the mediums who communicate with or channel them. Coined in 1894 by French physician and Spiritualist Charles Richet (1850–1935), winner of the 1913 Nobel Prize for Physiology and Medicine, the word derives from the Greek *ekto plasma*, meaning "outside substance" or "exterior substance." Ectoplasm is also sometimes called *mediumistic teleplastic*.

Ectoplasm may exude directly from a medium's body. The word may also be used to describe the white mist associated with the presence of ghosts. Not all mediums manifest ectoplasm, nor do all ghosts. One medium's ectoplasm may not be identical to another's. Ectoplasm may be a mist or vapor, but may also resemble thick fog or mucus. It is usually a white, sticky substance, but may also be other colors. Frequently described as smelling like ozone or smoldering electrical wires, ectoplasm can transform its shape to form entities or objects. Faces, hands, or even entire bodies may materialize. Ectoplasm, or what purports to be ectoplasm, frequently appears in spirit photographs.

Ectoplasm is exuded from a medium's body—usually, but not always, from the mouth. It may emanate from any orifice or even from pores. It allegedly disappears when exposed to light, retreating back into the medium's body. Touching ectoplasm or exposing it to light is said to be hazardous to a medium's health. For this reason, séances are often conducted in darkened rooms. Some mediums prefer to practice within closed cabinets. A famous exception is European medium Eva C., who manifested ectoplasm beneath a red light.

Exactly what constitutes ectoplasm, or even whether it really exists, is controversial. Researcher Gustave Géley (1868–1924), former director of the Institut Métaphysique International in Paris, suggested that ectoplasm might be related to a medium's doppelganger. It allegedly retains energy derived from a medium in action.

Ectoplasm is a mediumship phenomenon that is particularly easy to fake and many have been caught doing just that. Items used to produce fraudulent ectoplasm include regurgitated gauze, rubber gloves, muslin, cheesecloth, egg whites, gelatin, soap, peroxide, toothpaste, and paper. Phosphorus can provide an eerie glow. Because this phenomenon has been faked so often, many refuse to believe that genuine ectoplasm exists, although the imitators are mimicking *something*.

Eddy Brothers

William and Horatio Eddy came from a family long associated with the paranormal. A distant relative, Mary Bradley, was convicted of witchcraft in Salem, Massachusetts, but escaped from prison with the help of friends. The Eddy brothers' grandmother allegedly possessed second sight and spoke to invisible beings while in a deep trance. Their mother, Julia Maccombs, frightened her neighbors with her accurate prophesies. Their father, Zephaniah Eddy, a brutal man, accused her of being Satan's servant, and she learned to hide her ability to foretell the future.

The boys grew up on a farm near the town of Chittenden, in Vermont's Green Mountains. Their own psychic powers began to manifest when they were small

and in such a powerful fashion that they could not be hidden. They were seen playing with other small boys who vanished into thin air when anyone else approached. The Eddy boys fell into profoundly deep trances from which they could not be roused. The powers they manifested while entranced included accurate prophesy, levitation, and telekinesis. They sometimes vanished from within their house only to reappear mysteriously outside.

The boys were unable to attend school, as they attracted too much attention. In their presence, desks levitated and inkwells and other objects flew through the air. Horatio and William remained illiterate for the rest of their lives.

Their father attempted to beat their psychic powers out of them, but to no avail. When they fell into trance, he tried to rouse them with his fists or a rawhide whip. A Christian friend, who felt sorry for Zephaniah's plight, suggested he douse his sons with boiling water the next time they became entranced, but, although they were scalded, they did not waken. The same friend was permitted by Zephaniah to drop a red-hot coal into William's hand while he was entranced. The trance remained unbroken, but William bore the scar for the rest of his life.

At this stage of their lives, the Eddy boys demonstrated little control over their powers. They were unable to stop them manifesting, even though it brought such severe abuse. Sometimes spirits attempted to defend the boys. Perhaps out of fear as much as greed, Zephaniah Eddy sold his children to a traveling sideshow. The brothers spent the next fourteen years traveling through North America and Europe. They were treated as freaks, and beaten and abused daily.

Audiences were encouraged to try to break the boys' trances by throwing things at them. The boys were bound, gagged, and locked within spirit cabinets to see whether they could escape. Hot wax was poured into their mouths, and then they were challenged to produce spirit voices. Many in the audience genuinely believed that the boys were possessed by demons. They were stoned on more than one occasion. They had guns aimed at them, and had to be rescued from an angry mob in Danvers, Massachusetts, the renamed site of the original Salem Village. William was once ridden out of a town on a rail and just barely escaped being tarred and feathered.

In 1882, Zephaniah Eddy died and the boys returned to Vermont to live with their mother and sister, Mary, who became a practicing Spiritualist medium. They converted their home into a small inn, the Green Tavern. Chittenden evolved into a Spiritualist vacation hot spot. Guests traveled from around the globe to stay at the Eddys' inn. Although the family charged ten dollars for a week's room and board, a substantial sum at the time, séances were offered free to the public every day but Sunday. Crowds flocked to Chittenden and, as there were not enough rooms at the Eddy homestead to meet demand, tourists stayed with other local families, bringing a steady source of income to the town.

Guests at Green Tavern were allowed to roam the house freely. Many searched high and low for evidence that the Eddys were committing fraud. No evidence was ever found.

During their séances, one brother entered a spirit cabinet and fell into a trance. Lavish spiritual phenomena then began to manifest, including mysterious lights and noises. Musical instruments played by themselves. Spirits—as many as thirty at a time—emerged from the spirit cabinet. They prophesied, sang, and often spoke with audience members in foreign languages that the brothers almost certainly did not know. The brothers also demonstrated levitation, teleportation, and automatic writing.

The goings-on at Green Tavern attracted media attention. Prominent attorney, journalist, and veteran Henry Steel Olcott decided to investigate. He had previously served on the three-man commission that had investigated the assassination of Abraham Lincoln. Although he did not particularly like the Eddys, he became convinced that they were not frauds. While staying at Green Tavern, Olcott met another guest, Russian medium Helena Blavatsky, with whom he would eventually create an influential new spiritual movement, Theosophy.

Physically and emotionally scarred by years of incessant abuse, the Eddy brothers grew into surly, suspicious men, although Horatio sometimes performed magic tricks for neighboring children. Horatio died on September 8, 1922. William, a bitter recluse, lived another decade, dying on October 25, 1932 at ninety-nine.

If the elaborate séances produced at the Eddy home in Vermont were indeed fraudulent—as many who were not there insist that they must have been—then the family must have employed a huge cast. Where in their small house in their little Vermont town were all these accomplices hidden? Why did none ever come forward?

Edison, Thomas

Born February 11, 1847, Thomas Edison is an internationally recognized genius, scientist, and businessman who founded fourteen companies, including General Electric. Edison is considered among the most prolific inventors of all time, holding 1,093 United States patents in his own name. His inventions include the phonograph, the lightbulb, and the motion picture camera. Edison helped develop the electric chair and invented an entire integrated system of electrical lighting.

Edison built the very first industrial research laboratory in Menlo Park, New Jersey. (In 1954, the town's name was changed to Edison.) He conceived the principle of recording and reproducing sound between May and July 1877. When the phonograph first appeared in 1877, people were so amazed that they dubbed Edison the "Wizard of Menlo Park."

Edison's extensive, but less well known, paranormal pursuits are often expunged from his biographies. Many consider him to be among the fathers of paranormal investigation, his practical experiments fueled by his quest for communication with spirits.

Born in Ohio and raised in Port Huron, Michigan, Edison attended school for three months, but had trouble focusing. He was then homeschooled by his mother. He lost his hearing at an early age, possibly as a result of scarlet fever and recurring ear infections. As a teenager, he saved a three-year-old boy from a runaway train. The child's father, the station agent, was so thankful that he trained Edison as a telegraph operator.

Edison, convinced of the existence of spirits, was determined to construct a machine that would enable spirit/human communication. This was his initial motivation. He believed he could build an electronic device that could enable the living to speak with the dead. He theorized that this was possible because personality is stored within the brain's memory cells. Following death and decomposition, these memory cells retain a person's essence and are liberated into the atmosphere where they can be accessed. Edison believed new recording devices could contact the "living impaired," as he referred to the dead. He thought new technology could provide portals through which spirits could contact us. He sought to create devices that would be more sensitive, sophisticated, and reliable than mediums and spirit boards, which he perceived as crude.

Fascinated with spirit photography, Edison believed that it was possible for spirits to have their images captured on film. In the October 1920 issue of *Scientific American* magazine, Edison said that he was working on an electronic voice phenomena (EVP) device. He died on October 18, 1931 of complications from diabetes before the device was complete. No plans were left behind. Edison's last words, as reported by those present at his deathbed, were: "It is very beautiful over there."

Electromagnetic Field Meter (EMF meter)

EMF meters, also known as electromagnetic field detectors, are favorite tools of many ghost hunters, although that was not their initial purpose. Originally, EMF meters were designed to locate and measure artificial sources of electric and magnetic radiation. (Natural electromagnetic fields rarely fluctuate and are measured by specialized and far more expensive devices.) Common sources of man-made electromagnetic fields within buildings include cell phones, clock radios, televisions, and similar appliances and devices.

According to some theories, spirits may disrupt electromagnetic fields, or even possibly create their own. Thus, the meter may be used to help locate or identify their presence. No scientific evidence supports this belief—at least, not yet.

Others believe that minor fluctuations in electromagnetic fields can trigger hallucinations (or the susceptibility to hallucination) in some individuals, which may possibly cause them to think that they are experiencing paranormal activity. No scientific evidence supports this belief either.

Electronic Voice Phenomena (EVP)

What if the dead could speak to us directly, bypassing the need for mediums or Ouija boards? What if modern technology has created portals enabling the dead to do just that? Can the dead communicate with the living via electronic devices? Thomas Edison sought to create technology that would provide portals of communication for ghosts and other spirits. As early as the 1890s, he strove to initiate contact via an early phonograph device.

Electronic Voice Phenomena, or EVP, is an audio recording of a voice where no known or conventionally accepted source for that voice exists. EVPs are allegedly the voices of the dead, captured and preserved by modern technology. These voices are sometimes heard as they occur, but are usually unnoticed until the recording is played back. Essentially, many EVPs are unexplained audio events or unexpected voices found amid audio recordings.

EVP experiments have been conducted using a wide variety of devices, including old-fashioned tape recorders, digital voice recorders, audio and video recorders, video equipment, radios, telephones, televisions, microcassettes, microphones, cameras, computers, and answering machines.

Although EVP purports to be recordings of voices, they are often, but not always, garbled. Sometimes voices are clear, but often it takes effort (as well as wishful thinking, skeptics say) to recognize them as intelligible voices. Sometimes voices can be heard only by adjusting tape speeds. Some EVP voices address ghost hunters or others by name. Sometimes, EVP voices respond to questions in the manner of a Ouija board.

The concept of EVP descends from Edison's techno-spiritual philosophy and experiments. Many consider EVPs to be the most incontrovertible evidence that the human soul survives after the body dies. Spirit voices were allegedly first captured in 1938 on phonograph records, but the credit for discovering EVPs is usually given to Friedrich Jürgenson (1903–1987). For further details, see his entry on page 125.

One person's voice from beyond the grave is another's random radio signal or background noise. Skeptics suggest that EVPs are just random signals that people mistakenly interpret as meaningful. Of course, it is possible that Electronic Voice Phenomena are only meaningful to those for whom a message is meant or those with the skills and abilities to recognize and interpret these messages.

Extrasensory Perception (ESP)

Are humans limited to only five senses? Should anything beyond those five senses be considered paranormal? Extrasensory perception, or ESP, refers to perception or communication by means other than the five conventionally accepted physical senses: sight, hearing, taste, touch, and smell. ESP is the ability to apprehend what is beyond the capacity of these five senses. It is thus sometimes called "the sixth sense."

ESP has emerged as an umbrella term encompassing many forms of paranormal psychic phenomena, including clairvoyance, telepathy, clairaudience, and precognition.

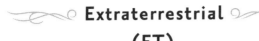

Extraterrestrial
(ET)

Is Earth the only inhabited planet? Are the indigenous inhabitants of Earth (people, birds, animals, fish, insects) the only living creatures in the whole universe? Extraterrestrials are beings whose origins lie beyond our planet.

The concept of extraterrestrials is ancient. In the distant past, many assumed that other planets were inhabited. Myths and legends describe deities who lived on the Moon and other celestial bodies. In recent decades, however, there has been growing anxiety about the existence of extraterrestrials. Are they out there? Are they really visiting us and, if so, why? Are they here to save us, enslave us, or harvest us? In Steven Spielberg's 1982 blockbuster film *ET, The Extraterrestrial*, the lonely little alien just wants to phone home. That movie brought the possibility of extraterrestrial life, once a fringe topic, to a mass audience.

Some theorize that extraterrestrials have been visiting Earth for millions of years in order to help humanity evolve. Some believe that ancient astronauts visited Earth in the distant past and were responsible for seeding the Earth with humans. Others believe that extraterrestrials are our ancestors. Yet others perceive them as predatory intruders bent on dominating or even destroying us.

Many people claim to have had personal encounters with extraterrestrials. Some of these experiences are described as terrifying, while others are characterized as positive. Perhaps not everyone is encountering the same extraterrestrials. Several different types have been described. The following are among the most prevalent, but other types are also described, including extraterrestrials that resemble giant praying mantises.

Greys, so named for the color of their skin, are intelligent beings apparently more technologically and scientifically advanced than we are. Greys are humanoid in appearance with large heads and eyes, small bodies, and thin limbs. They account for a significant proportion of purported alien encounters in North America, but are less well-known elsewhere. A fictional example of a Grey is Roger from the animated television series, *American Dad*.

Nordics are so called because they allegedly resemble humans of Northern European extraction. They look very much like humans, more so than Greys or Reptilians. Nordics are described as very white-skinned with white or pale blond hair and blue eyes, although some are described as having pink, violet, red, or yellow eyes. Sometimes called Pleiadeans after the Pleiades star cluster, Nordics play a substantial role in abduction and contactee lore from Europe and Latin America, but are comparatively rare among accounts from the United States and Canada.

Reptilians, also known as Reptoids, are comparable in size to humans, but possess the scaly skin and snout-like facial features of a snake or lizard. Reptilian humanoids appear frequently in mythology and some perceive a connection between these ancient myths and modern UFO lore. Examples include the half-man/half-snake Cecrops, first king of Athens, and Quetzalcoatl, the Aztec plumed serpent. Some even associate Reptilian aliens with the talking snake in the Garden of Eden. Reptilians are considered intelligent, predatory aliens. Some claim that they originated on Earth and now seek to reclaim this planet because conditions in their present home have deteriorated.

Extraterrestrial Highway

Because it is the site of many alleged UFO sightings and because of its proximity to Area 51, Nevada State Highway 375 was officially renamed the Extraterrestrial Highway in April 1996. The Extraterrestrial Highway stretches for ninety-eight miles. Strange lights are often reported by those driving along this road at night, although whether these are attributable to alien spacecraft or secret military aircraft is subject to debate.

The Extraterrestrial Highway runs through a remote area. If you drive it, make sure you have plenty of drinking water as well as fluids for your car. Other than several ranches, the town of Rachel is the only settlement along the highway. However, many historic sites—including old mines, ghost towns, and the natural hot mineral springs at Warm Springs—are easily reached via this route, and it has become a popular tourist destination. The Little A'Le'Inn in Rachel welcomes Earthlings. Most of the highway runs through open range, meaning that there are no fences, and one is more likely to see cattle on the road than extraterrestrials. It is crucial to be especially careful when driving there at night, as cows on the road may not be easily visible.

Fort, Charles

A 1941 *New York Times* review described Charles Fort as "the enfant terrible of science, bringing the family skeletons to the dinner table." Considered the leading pioneer of paranormal studies, Charles Fort was so influential that his name has entered the English language as an adjective: strange and extraordinary phenomenon and happenings are now defined as "Fortean."

Born in Albany, New York in 1874, Charles Hoy Fort moved to New York City in 1892 where he found work as a newspaper reporter. He traveled the world for several years before marrying in 1896 and returning to New York. Meanwhile, Fort had begun compulsively collecting and cataloging odd stories and anecdotes—interesting anomalies that lacked conventional explanation; phenomena that would eventually be classified as "paranormal." His first book, *The Book of the Damned*, was compiled from notes he had written on 40,000 slips of paper and stuffed into shoeboxes.

Fort introduced a revolutionary new topic, and publishers did not quite know what to make of him. His writing career was encouraged by Theodore Dreiser, author of the controversial 1900 novel *Sister Carrie*. Dreiser, who became Fort's closest friend, was working as an editor at Street and Smith, publishers of pulp fiction. *The Book of the Damned* was only published because Dreiser threatened to leave his own publisher if they didn't take it.

Those reading his first book and expecting something demonic will be disappointed. The title of *The Book of the Damned* refers to data or information that has been "damned" or excluded by science because it doesn't fit accepted guidelines. According to Fort, science constructs theories by ignoring inconvenient facts. He compared the closed-mindedness of many scientists to religious fundamentalists and suggested that science had become a *de facto* religion with its own ideology and dogma.

Fort wrote seven books, of which only four survive. They have now been collected into one volume and republished as *The Book of the Damned: The Collected Works of Charles Fort* (Jeremy P. Tarcher/Penguin Books, 2008). He was among the first to discuss alien abductions. A shy, reclusive man, Fort died in 1932 following a lengthy illness, most likely leukemia. The monthly *Fortean Times Magazine* was founded in 1973 with the intent of continuing Fort's work.

Fox Sisters

March 31, 1848, the birthday of modern Spiritualism, commemorates the date when Maggie and Kate Fox first made contact with the rambunctious spirit haunting their home. The Fox family had moved into a rented cottage in Hydesville, near Rochester in upper New York State on December 11, 1847. Almost immediately, they heard loud, disembodied raps, thumps, and knocks coming from floors, walls, and ceilings all over the little house. It made them nervous, and they complained to neighbors.

There are three Fox sisters associated with Spiritualism, but only two were in the house on that momentous Friday. Margaret (Maggie) was fourteen, and Kate (also sometimes spelled Cathie or Katy) was eleven. They were the youngest of six children of blacksmith John Fox and his wife, Margaret, whose family was reputedly gifted with second sight. After months of strange noises, the family's nerves were shot. They searched for the source of these sounds, but were unable to find it. Kate nicknamed the mysterious noise-maker "Mr. Splitfoot," a nickname for the devil, perhaps because he bedeviled them.

On March 31, the sounds began in the daytime. Constant loud rapping, thumping, and knocking continued through the night, until finally Kate clapped her hands three times, saying: "Mr. Splitfoot, do as I do." Instantly, three answering raps were heard. Kate repeated her clapping, and the house echoed them back. When she was quiet, the house was quiet, too. Maggie then cried out: "Do as I do! Count one, two, three, four!" Clapping rhythmically four times, she received echoing raps in return.

Mr. Fox went to get neighbors to come witness these strange events. Mary Redfield agreed to accompany him, although she originally assumed, as did other neighbors, that it was only an elaborate, early April Fools' trick. Instead, she discovered the three Fox females huddled together in the girls' bedroom. Loud knocking noises came from the walls.

Mrs. Fox asked the spirit to rap out the ages of her children. The phantom did so, pausing between each child. In addition to her living children, the phantom also rapped out the age of another who had died years before at age three. Few were aware of the existence of this child, convincing Mrs. Fox that she was communicating with a real spirit. When Mrs. Fox asked it to tap out Mary Redfield's age, the phantom accurately knocked thirty-three times.

The Fox family began to ask questions using a system of one rap for "yes" and two for "no." They asked permission to invite other neighbors. The spirit assented, and neighbors came and stayed for hours. By the next day, the Fox sisters and the spirit had worked out a system that assigned numbers to letters of the alphabet, thereby enabling more complex communication. By that night, 300 people had crowded into the cottage to witness the spirit communicating with the Fox sisters, revealing information that these young, unsophisticated, barely educated girls could not have known on their own.

The spirit identified himself as Charles Rosma, a peddler, and described his murder in the house approximately five years earlier. Rosma had called at the cottage, then occupied by Mr. and Mrs. John Bell. The Bells cut his throat with a butcher knife, stole his cash ($500, he claimed, a substantial sum at that time), and bricked his body up behind a basement wall. It was his ghost haunting the cottage, seeking justice and driving out the tenants who had lived there before the Foxes— a young couple named Weekman. The Weekmans later confirmed that they had indeed left the cottage because they were spooked by constant strange noises. A woman who had been employed by the Bells also confirmed some details of the story. Mr. and Mrs. Bell threatened to sue for defamation of character.

Several people, led by the son, David Fox, searched the basement for evidence. They dug down three feet, but hit water and had to stop. (The spring of 1848 was unusually wet.) They made another attempt in July and, although they hit water again, this time they found bone fragments and strands of hair. Skeptics claimed these came from animals.

Only in 1904 was the truth discovered. The east wall of the cellar of the now abandoned cottage collapsed, almost killing some children playing there. A man who came to their rescue realized that the collapsed wall was a shoddily constructed false partition. A male skeleton was discovered between the false brick wall and the original cellar wall, along with a large box resembling those carried by peddlers. The skeleton was never identified conclusively. Were these the remains of Charles Rosma, as the mysterious rapping had claimed? If the Fox sisters were charlatans, as many believe, how did they know of the existence of this skeleton?

Following the events of March 31, 1848, the Hydesville cottage was inundated by visitors and media. Although the news of the phenomenon triggered Spiritualism elsewhere, the local attention it garnered was generally not pleasant. While some perceived what had occurred as incontrovertible proof of life after death, many reacted with open hostility. Neighbors accused the Fox family of practicing witchcraft. Within a few weeks, they were expelled from the Methodist church they attended, and accused of blasphemy and devil worship. Mrs. Fox's hair turned white literally overnight.

Hostility in Hydesville drove the girls from home. They were sent to live with relatives. Kate went to a brother, while Maggie was sent to their sister, Leah, in Rochester. Although separated, the rapping phenomenon—and more!—followed them. Both girls were terrorized by poltergeists that stuck them with pins and threw blocks of wood at them. Only when they resumed their spirit communications did this harassment end, corresponding with traditional beliefs about shamanism, which the Foxes, staunch Methodists, likely did not know. If spirits wish to communicate with you, shamans believe, they will pursue you until you acquiesce.

In 1848, Leah, eldest of the Fox children, was thirty-five years old, twenty-one years older than Maggie, the elder of the two rapping sisters. When Leah was fourteen, she had married Bowman Fish and bore a daughter shortly after. Fish abruptly abandoned his wife and child, but Leah did not return home to her family as advised. An enterprising woman, she lived independently, supporting herself and her little girl by giving piano lessons. Now, her parents gave her charge of both younger sisters as well.

The media was enthralled with the pretty young Fox sisters. They became celebrities, yet were desperately poor. The scandal caused Leah to lose her piano students. Parents didn't want their children in contact with such a notorious woman. She literally had no income. In 1850, Leah suggested that, instead of allowing an endless parade of strangers into her home, they should book a theater for a night. This turned into a great success.

The girls went on tour accompanied by Leah, who served as their medium and manager. Leah Fox is often considered the first official modern Spiritualist medium. She decided to charge an admission fee of one dollar per person for their séances. By the early

1850s, they were earning between $100 and $150 a day. They never changed their rates substantially. Even at the height of their popularity when they could have charged more, Leah still only charged one dollar per person to attend their séances, less than some other mediums. Newspaper publisher Horace Greeley advised her to raise prices to ensure a higher-class clientele and keep the riffraff out, but Leah refused. Greeley introduced them to high society. Among those attending their séances were Greeley, poet William Cullen Bryant, author James Fenimore Cooper (*The Last of the Mohicans*), and abolitionists William Lloyd Garrison and Sojourner Truth.

The three sisters developed mediumship and could communicate with other spirits. Although the media dubbed them the Rochester Rappers, the Fox sisters were not limited to rapping. Maggie and Kate also demonstrated healing powers. Kate reputedly was able to provide relief for Elizabeth Cady Stanton's brother-in-law, homeopathic physician Edward Bayer, who suffered from neuralgia.

Kate is generally considered the most gifted of the three. George and Sarah Taylor, at the Swedish Movement Cure Hospital where she was repeatedly treated for alcoholism and where she sometimes presided over séances, compiled 1367 spirit communications delivered by Kate over twenty-three years, including messages from their own two dead children. Their surviving son, William Taylor, described Kate as "a great medium—all classes of spirits, high and low, elect and damned, could manifest through her channel."

Although some welcomed contact with spirits, the Fox sisters were always controversial. Their tale is not one of gullible audiences. From the very start, the girls were under suspicion and extensively tested. The goal of the tests was not to exonerate them, but to prove that they were frauds. People were convinced they were charlatans. The rumor that they were producing phenomena by loudly cracking their joints and popping their toes dogged them.

In November 1849, the Fox sisters were tested by a panel of investigators. No fraud was detected—*not* the desired result of the investigation—so a second investigation was demanded with brand-new investigators. Again, no fraud was detected. This testing did not stop, but continued throughout their careers. The girls presented mediumistic phenomena barefoot, standing on pillows, and with their long skirts tied around their ankles. Women were brought in to strip-search them, making the modest young girls cry, but no devices were found. No one ever debunked the Fox sisters, despite tremendous efforts and extensive testing.

Money collected for séances created a wedge between the sisters. Maggie especially resented Leah's control over their finances, although Leah housed, clothed, fed, and otherwise cared for her siblings.

Maggie fell madly in love with Arctic explorer Dr. Elisha Kane, a media hero and scion of a rich,

elegant mainline Philadelphia family. Kane attempted
to mold Maggie into someone more acceptable to
his family. He sent her to school, encouraging her to
gain an education, but also pressured her to abandon
mediumship. In the 19th century, it was not respectable for women to be employed, especially not in such
a controversial profession. Maggie Fox was essentially
a performer who put on stage shows for a paying audience. Maggie and Elisha may have secretly married,
although the validity of their marriage was later called
into question. By 1853, Maggie had withdrawn from
mediumship.

On August 15, 1858, Maggie was baptized a
Roman Catholic. Elisha, although a Presbyterian, pressured her to embrace Catholicism, possibly because it
strictly forbade adherents from raising spirits of the
dead. Meanwhile, Leah married her third husband,
David Underwood, and Kate traveled alone to Europe,
where she was tested by prominent psychic researchers
who were unable to discover anything fraudulent.

Elisha and Maggie never lived together. He died far from her. Although he allegedly left her a bequest in his will, his family did not acknowledge Maggie, and she did not receive what she thought had been promised to her. This left her in dire financial straits. Following Elisha's death, she began drinking heavily. Kate, widowed with two sons, began drinking with her. Tremendous tension existed between Maggie and Leah, while Kate maintained relations with both her sisters.

In 1885, Leah Fox Underwood wrote a book, *The Missing Link in Modern Spiritualism*, intended to promote Spiritualism. In 1888, Maggie contracted with journalist Reuben Briggs Davenport to write her memoir, entitled *The Death-Blow to Spiritualism*, in which she denounced Spiritualism as fraud, claiming that Leah had forced her younger sisters to serve as mediums.

On October 21, 1888, Maggie publicly testified against Spiritualism at New York's Academy of Music, a 3,000-seat theater. Confessing that she was a fraud, she demonstrated how she had made clicking noises with her toes. This did little to halt the controversy. Those already convinced that mediums were charlatans felt vindicated. Others reacted with pity and anger, discounting Maggie's confession.

Maggie's bitter hatred for Leah was cited as the stimulus for her confession, while Spiritualist Isaac Funk, publisher of Funk and Wagnall's encyclopedias, suggested that Maggie was so desperate for money that for five dollars she would have sworn to anything.

In fact, Maggie had been promised a speaking tour of the United States in which she would preach against Spiritualism. A dispute about her compensation, however, caused the tour to be cancelled.

Kate was at Maggie's side at the Academy of Music, but remained silent, causing many to assume that she had tacitly confessed to fraud as well. Kate later said that she did not anticipate Maggie's testimony and did not agree with it, but could not publicly contradict her beloved sister. By 1889, Maggie had recanted her confession.

Leah was very depressed by Maggie's testimony. On November 1, 1890, she died of a stroke in New York City at seventy-four. On July 1, 1892, Kate, fifty-six, died as a result of advanced alcoholism. In the winter of 1892–93, Maggie, critically ill and bedridden in her New York tenement, was attended by a non-Spiritualist physician from the Medico Legal Society, who spent several hours with her daily. According to the physician, although Maggie could no longer move her hands or feet and the apartment possessed no closets or similar hiding places, knocks and raps were heard continuously.

On March 5, 1893, a notice appeared on the back page of the *New York Times*:

Margaret Fox Kane Destitute

Margaret Fox Kane, one of the Fox sisters . . . is sick and destitute at the rooms she has long been occupying at the tenement house [at] 456 West Fifty-Seventh Street. Though she is very ill, she will be

dispossessed on Tuesday. Titus Merritt . . . is taking
up a subscription among his friends with a view to
sending Mrs. Kane to some sort of sanitarium.

Maggie died homeless on March 8, 1893 at fifty-nine.
Both Maggie and Kate died penniless alcoholics. If
Maggie's confession was true and the sisters began as
frauds, did the experience in Hydesville and its after-
math awaken their latent psychic skills? Those who have
attempted to replicate the trick as described by Maggie
have consistently demonstrated disappointing results.
For more information, see *The Reluctant Spiritualist: The
Life of Maggie Fox* by Nancy Rubin Stuart. The Elisha
Kent Kane Historical Society (*www.ekkane.org/sawin/
sawin.htm#contents*) contains a lengthy description of the
romance between Maggie Fox and the hero explorer, as
well as their letters.

 Ghost Club

Despite its name, the Ghost Club is not a place where
Casper the Ghost can raise a glass with Harry Potter's
Nearly Headless Nick—or at least, not officially.
Instead, the Ghost Club is believed to be the very old-
est society for paranormal research and investigation.
It is a nonprofit social club run by an elected council of
volunteers.

The roots of the Ghost Club lie in England's
Trinity College where, in 1855, some fellows began

serious discussion of ghosts and other psychic phenomena. Founded in London in 1862, the club's primary interest is paranormal activity associated with ghosts and hauntings. Author Charles Dickens was among its earliest members. The Ghost Club was dormant for several years following Dickens' death, but then revived on November 1, 1882. Other famous members have included poet William Butler Yeats, author Arthur Koestler (*Darkness at Noon*), and Hammer horror film star, actor Peter Cushing.

In conjunction with historic houses, heritage sites, and unusual locations, the Ghost Club hosts paranormal investigations with the intent of conducting serious research. Although based in the United Kingdom, its membership is international. According to their website, interested skeptics are welcome. For more information, go to *www.ghostclub.org.uk*.

Ghosts

Does the human soul survive death? Ghosts are generally acknowledged to be the spirits or souls of dead people. (For exceptions, see Poltergeist; Stone Tape Theory.) Traditional cultures offer different explanations of what happens after death. However, the concept of the revenant, the returning soul of someone no longer living, is acknowledged by all human cultures.

Surviving ancient texts from China, Egypt, Greece, and elsewhere reveal a fascination with ghosts. Indeed, ghost stories exist everywhere. In Homer's *Odyssey*, Odysseus undergoes a shamanic journey to Hades, expertly guided by the sorceress-goddess, Circe. *The Instruction of Amenemhet* consists of guidance from the ghost of a 12th-dynasty pharaoh for his son and successor regarding how to govern and whom to trust (*no one!*). Who wrote the *Instruction of Amenemhet?* It may have been written during the reign of his son or later and the format may be nothing more than a literary device. Or it may, as claimed, have been channeled by a medium or actually received from the king's ghost.

Although some cultures take the presence of ghosts in stride, others find them profoundly disturbing for a variety of reasons. This is especially so in religions where souls are supposed to depart this mortal coil and transition to another realm—Heaven, Hell, Hades, Avalon, Valhalla, or elsewhere. Ghosts are equally disturbing in cultures where souls are expected to reincarnate. Why do ghosts linger among us? What keeps them earthbound? Many possible explanations are offered, including:

- The ghost is not aware that she or he is dead.
- Somehow trapped on the earthly plane, the ghost is unable to transition.
- The ghost has unfinished business, perhaps a message to be delivered or justice to be sought.
- Love.
- Lack of proper (or any) funeral arrangements.

There is also a traditional belief in many cultures that those who die in certain circumstances are fated to transform into powerful ghosts, whether benevolent or malevolent. For example, in traditional Japanese culture, women who die while feeling intensely negative emotions—rage or jealousy, for instance—may transform into malevolent ghosts known as *Hannya*, while in Latin America, murder victims, especially young women, may evolve into saintly miracle workers called *Almitas*.

The existence of ghosts was once accepted as natural, and many people claim to have had personal experience of them. Modern, science-oriented societies, however, ridicule this belief in ghosts. Paranormal societies, thus, focus on proving the existence of ghosts in a scientific manner.

Is there an invisible world of ghosts and spirits that exists, but has not yet been proven scientifically? To put this in context, consider electricity, gravity, magnetism, radioactivity, radio waves, cell phone signals, and television frequencies. All are invisible, yet now acknowledged as real. Centuries ago, all would have been considered fantastic and untrue. Of course, we know gravity, magnetism, television frequencies, and the rest by their effects and what they produce. We can experience them even if we can't see them. Is it possible that ghosts are similar phenomena? Do ghosts possess their own frequencies or signals? Some theorize that ghosts exert a measure of control over magnetic fields. And, in fact, some ghost hunters attempt to identify the presence of ghosts conclusively using EMF or EVP devices.

Various indications suggest the presence of ghosts. Sensitive people may experience feelings of oppression or danger, the presence of malevolence, or an unshakeable feeling of being watched by invisible eyes. Others experience sudden feelings of apprehension, including physical reactions like goose bumps and raised hackles. A ghostly encounter can literally be a hair-raising experience. Animals may refuse to enter a haunted room, house, or area.

All of these indications may also signal some other type of spirit manifestation. Two indications, however, are associated virtually exclusively with ghosts: a sudden, otherwise inexplicable, temperature drop and candles that burn with low, dull flames. (Other types of spirit manifestations are often characterized by high, bright, jumping flames.)

There are many different types of ghosts. Not every haunted house shelters the same type of entity. Some ghosts remain invisible. Their presence may only be felt or possibly heard. Some ghosts signal their presence with a distinct aroma. The scent of cigarettes or perfume may mysteriously appear without apparent cause, for instance.

Other ghosts are visible and instantly recognizable as supernatural. The classic ghost is a shadowy, gauzy apparition. Some ghosts, however, are so tangible and substantial that they are easily mistaken for  the living, given away for what they are only when they vanish into thin air or walk right through a solid wall or locked door.

An example of a tangible ghost is the famous Highland Ghost who haunts Scotland's Stirling Castle. He derives his nickname from his traditional highlander's garb. The Highland Ghost roams Stirling Castle and appears so vital that tourists frequently mistake him for a tour guide in period dress. Much to their annoyance, however, when they try to obtain directions or speak with him, he walks away as if ignoring them. Only when the Highland Ghost walks through a wall or a closed door do they realize that they have seen a ghost.

Some ghosts manifest in unusual ways. Allegedly, the ghost of Lady Mary Berkeley roams the halls of England's Chillingham Castle searching for her wayward husband, who abandoned her in the castle after running off with her sister. Visitors to the haunted castle, which offers ghost tours, report feeling cold spots and hearing the rustle of long skirts. Lady Mary has occasionally been seen stepping out of her portrait in the nursery and seems to enjoy terrifying children by following them.

Some ghosts deliver warnings, while the very appearance of others is a harbinger of disaster or misfortune. In other words, if you can see them, something bad is about to happen. A classic example is the Green Lady of Scotland's much-haunted Stirling Castle, site of the 1543 coronation of Mary, Queen of Scots. Rumor has it that, in life, the Green Lady served as Queen Mary's lady-in-waiting. She awoke abruptly one night from a nightmare in which her queen was in danger. Racing into the queen's bedchamber, she discovered the bed curtains on fire. The Green Lady managed to save her queen, but lost her own life in the process. Now her ghost appears whenever trouble is brewing at Stirling, especially fires. Her appearance is a warning to castle staff to be extra vigilant.

Although many claim to fear ghosts, ghost-hunting television programs have become increasingly popular, as have ghost tours that feature haunted houses or other sites allegedly haunted by ghosts. Once upon a time, hauntings were kept secret, but in the 21st century, they have evolved into promotional assets. People once fled from haunted houses. Now the same houses are converted into hotels, and guests are disappointed if they do not personally witness paranormal phenomena.

Hill,
Barney and Betty

Barney and Betty Hill claimed that, on the night of September 19–20, 1961, they were abducted by aliens. Theirs is considered the first documented account of alien abduction and was the first to be considered seriously by a wide audience. This is partially because the Hills initially resisted publicizing their case so that it was not easy to label them as attention seekers. The Hills also gained credibility because, other than their claims of alien abduction, they were widely perceived as being regular, *normal*, upstanding citizens.

Early on September 17, 1961, Barney and Betty Hill left their Portsmouth, New Hampshire home for a belated honeymoon. Although they had married almost sixteen months earlier, on May 12, 1960, professional commitments had kept them living apart for the first ten months of their marriage. It was a second marriage for both Hills. Forty-one-year-old Betty was a child social worker for the State of New Hampshire. Barney was a thirty-nine-year-old U.S. postal carrier in Philadelphia. In March 1961, he received a job transfer to Boston so that they were finally able to live together, although Barney had a grueling sixty-mile commute. Unable to spend as much time together as they desired, the couple took a few days off in September. The third member of their party was their dachshund, Delsey.

Driving a 1957 black-and-white Chevy Bel Air, the Hills traveled to Vermont, Niagara Falls, and Toronto before heading toward Montreal on September 19. They took a wrong turn, got lost in city traffic, and then were unable to decipher directions given to them in French. In addition, Barney was concerned about potential negative reactions to an interracial couple, a very valid concern in 1961. He kept driving, hoping to find a motel that would accept pets—and them!

When the Hills heard a radio broadcast announcing the approach of tropical storm Esther, they decided to return home early.  While driving through New Hampshire's White Mountains late that night, they noticed a bright object in the sky with an erratic flight pattern that seemed to be following them. The strange behavior of this silent craft caused the Hills to keep their collective eye on it as they traveled Route 3 through the Franconia Notch mountain pass. Barney suggested that it was a satellite; Betty rejected this. They described the craft as being at least as large as a four-engine plane.

The Hills arrived home at five in the morning, at least two hours later than they should have, although they were initially unaware of this. Both their watches had stopped working, and they did not realize this gap of missing time until they saw their clock at home. They were stunned. Between two and three hours of travel time was unaccounted for. What did the Hills do during those missing hours? Why had the trip taken so long? The Hills lacked answers to those questions, and it bothered them. Over two hours were missing from their memories. Both Hills were unable to recall where they had been or what they had done or witnessed. The last thing they remembered was hearing a beep and then driving home in a subdued mood. The strange, silent aircraft they had previously witnessed was no longer visible.

Although they had amnesia regarding those missing hours, they were well aware of other mysteries. When she arrived home, Betty discovered that her dress was torn, although she did not recall how or when it had happened. The tops of Barney's shoes, as opposed to the soles, were severely scraped, yet he could not remember how this had occurred. Both Hills had felt unclean on their arrival home and had taken showers. They did not, however, bathe Delsey, who quickly developed a severe fungal condition.

Barney soon developed twenty-one lesions in a perfect circle pattern on his groin. He wanted them removed. The first skin specialist he consulted refused to remove them, as he had never seen anything like them before. He referred Barney to another specialist, who removed them but was unable to identify them. They resembled warts, but, once removed and biopsied, they were found *not* to be warts and were never definitively diagnosed.

The Hills were convinced that they had encountered a UFO and that something strange had happened, but at this point, they did not consciously recall being abducted. Although Barney, who wished to keep their experiences private, tried to persuade her not to make the phone call, on September 21, 1951, Betty reported witnessing a UFO to the 100th Bombardment Wing at Pease Air Force Base in nearby Newington, New Hampshire. The air force allegedly confirmed that a UFO sighting had been made on the night in question, but did not offer further information.

On September 23, Betty borrowed the book *The Flying Saucer Conspiracy* from the library. Written by Major Donald Keyhoe, director of the National Investigation Committee on Aerial Phenomena, the book, published in 1955, suggests that the United States government suppresses UFO information. The book contained an address to which people could write if they had witnessed anything. Betty did just that. She was soon contacted by Keyhoe, as well as other researchers.

Ten days after their return, Betty began suffering recurrent nightmares. They disturbed her so much that she wrote them down, trying to place events in her dreams into some sort of sequential order. In her dreams, the Hills' car was stopped and surrounded by human-like beings. They were taller than Betty, who was 5'4" and had grayish skin with bluish lips and wore uniforms. These beings brought the Hills to a clearing in the woods and onto a disk-like aircraft where the Hills were subjected to medical examinations. Their skin was scraped, their hair and nails were clipped, and earwax was removed.

Seeking answers to these personal mysteries, the Hills began attending the meetings of a local UFO society. Prior to this, they had had absolutely no interest in UFOs. They did not watch *The Twilight Zone*, nor did they view Martian-oriented science fiction movies, as some have accused them of doing. Instead, their shared passion was civil rights, which was directly relevant to their own lives as an interracial couple in 1960s America.

On Sunday, November 3, 1963, they attended a UFO society meeting in Quincy, Massachusetts whose scheduled agenda included discussion of the validity of UFO sightings. The Hills went hoping to have their own questions regarding missing time and Betty's still-recurrent nightmares answered. Instead, they found themselves giving their first (impromptu) public presentation about their experiences to an audience of roughly 200 people. The audience sat riveted, but lacked answers to the Hills' concerns. The upshot was that the Hills' privacy and anonymity were now gone. Attendees taped the presentation, including the Hills' talk, without the Hills' knowledge or permission.

Both Barney and Betty were active members of the Unitarian Church and the NAACP. Barney, a prominent member of the NAACP, served on its board of directors, as well as on the United States Civil Rights Commission. Betty was active in the local Democratic Party. Both worked on voter registration. They did *not* court publicity, but were torn between protecting their privacy and seeking information.

Within a year of that September night, Barney's health declined dramatically. He suffered severe hypertension, insomnia, and migraines, as well as ulcers that failed to respond to medical treatment. He was forced to take a three-month leave of absence from the post office. Both Hills continued to experience debilitating anxiety attacks. Eventually, they decided to undergo hypnosis to relieve this anxiety and their double amnesia. They were referred to Dr. Benjamin Simon, a highly respected Boston psychiatrist and neurologist, who interviewed both Hills and diagnosed them with anxiety syndrome.

Their first hypnosis session was scheduled for January 4, 1964. Treatment terminated at the end of June 1964. Barney and Betty were hypnotized individually. Neither was initially informed what the other had revealed under hypnotic regression, but their stories largely corroborated each other.

Under hypnosis, Barney described the craft as resembling a big pancake with windows and lights. Its flight was totally silent. Barney stopped the car and tried to get a better look using binoculars. Putting Delsey on her leash and walking into a field where the view was better, Barney could see beings in the craft looking back at him. He ran back to the car where Betty was waiting and drove away. But, as if obeying unspoken directions, he turned down a remote side road where five humanoid figures blocked their path. The Hills were surrounded, removed from their car, and taken prisoner. Barney resisted capture more than Betty and was dragged to the aircraft, explaining how the tops of his shoes were scraped. Once on the aircraft, the couple was separated. While being examined, aliens placed some sort of cup over Barney's groin, corresponding to the twenty-one lesions that formed a circle.

Under hypnosis, Betty described the aliens as hairless with no earlobes or cartilage, only ear holes. She compared their noses to that of actor, Jimmy Durante. Contrary to the then-popular stereotype, her aliens were not little green men, but were aluminum gray in color with big chests and spindly legs. Betty described undergoing medical procedures. During her exam, a four- to six-inch needle

was inserted into her navel causing excruciating pain. She was informed that this was a pregnancy test. In the 1960s, many scoffed at this, but it is now reminiscent of laparoscopies or amniocentesis, a routine medical procedure to determine the genetic markers of a fetus. Amniocentesis was in the experimental stage in 1961 and not generally known in 1964.

The aliens apparently paid little attention to the difference in the Hills' skin color—Barney was black; Betty was white—but were fascinated by the discrepancy in their teeth. Barney's were removable and Betty's were not. Barney wore a full set of dentures following injuries incurred during his military service.

Under hypnosis, Betty reproduced a star map she said had been shown to her by her captors. Betty was no astronomer, and yet she drew an accurate map, including the location of two stars, Zeta I and Zeta II Reticuli, allegedly the home base of her aliens. The existence of these two stars was not confirmed by astronomers until 1969. Furthermore, these two fifth-magnitude stars are not visible north of Mexico City.

Betty had found a book featuring strange hiero-glyphs on the aircraft that she wanted to keep as a souvenir and as proof of her experience. The alien she identified as the leader agreed, but was later overruled by the crew, who did not wish their victims to be able to recall their experiences. The book was taken from her, and Betty was advised by the "leader" that the Hills' memories would be erased.

Betty insisted that she *would* remember, and the leader laughed at her, saying that, even if she did, Barney wouldn't. And in the event that he did, their memories would not correspond. They would confuse each other, and no one else would ever believe them. Barney revealed under hypnosis that he had been warned never to discuss his experiences. The aliens would allegedly know and would return to punish the Hills.

Dr. Simon, the hypnotist, very adamantly did *not* believe in alien abductions. It is unlikely that he hypnotically implanted these memories, as some have suggested. If anything, he attempted to dissuade the Hills of the possibility of alien abduction. Simon was willing to acknowledge the possibility of UFO sightings, but abductions were too much for him.

To the Hills' dismay, a newspaper reporter contacted them, seeking an interview and advising them that a newspaper story about their UFO experience was planned. Barney immediately contacted two lawyers in an attempt to force the newspaper publisher, editor, and reporter to withdraw the story. The lawyers informed him, however, that as long as medical confidentiality was not violated and the story was treated as news, nothing could be done to prevent publication.

In October 1965, the *Boston Traveler* ran a five-day series about the Hills. The first headline trumpeted, "UFO Chiller—Did They Seize Couple?" The newspaper plunged the Hills into the public eye. The reporter had questioned Betty's close friends, as well as members of their UFO research organization. He also obtained their Project Blue Book file and other suppos-

edly confidential documents. The newspaper sold its greatest number of copies in its eighty-four-year history.

The media surrounded the Hills' home and workplaces. Their telephone rang off the hook. Finally, the Hills agreed to speak publicly about their experience for the first time, appearing on Sunday, November 7, 1965 at Pierce Memorial Church in Dover, New Hampshire.

In 1966, *Look Magazine* featured the Hills in two articles. They became the face of UFO abductions, the very first case to become familiar to the general public. Their abduction saga was the subject of John Fuller's 1966 best-selling book, *The Interrupted Journey: Two Lost Hours "Aboard a Flying Saucer,"* featuring an introduction by Dr. Simon. Fuller was perceived as a "serious author," not a crackpot. His was the first book to make a serious case that individuals were being abducted by aliens.

The Hills shared royalties with Fuller. The book did not make them rich, but made enough money so that they could live more comfortably. They traded in the Chevy they had driven that fateful night for an Oldsmobile. The story of the Hills' abduction was made into the 1975 television movie, *The UFO Incident*, starring James Earl Jones and Estelle Parsons.

The health of all three passengers in the car that night deteriorated dramatically. In June 1967, Betty was hospitalized with pericarditis, an inflammation of the pericardium, the sac-like covering around the heart. Polyps on her vocal chords were removed surgically in 1968, leaving her unable to speak above a whisper. Although her voice eventually returned, it was never the same. During her treatment, she discovered that many records had vanished from her medical file. On December 24, 1968, Delsey died unexpectedly following a bladder infection and dehydration that would not respond to veterinary care. On February 25, 1969, Barney died of a cerebral hemorrhage at age forty-six.

Following Barney's death, Betty became more involved with UFO societies and was among the best-known spokespeople for UFO research, although her health continued to suffer. By 1975, she was experiencing crippling episodes of back, chest, and head pain, accompanied by loss of balance, profuse sweating, and tremors. Forced to retire at fifty-six, she became more active with UFO groups, surrounding herself with UFO enthusiasts.

Betty wrote that she and Barney did not believe in ghosts, but did believe in extraterrestrial life and travel. Anxious to reestablish contact with aliens and to obtain physical proof of their existence and her experience, she engaged in several experiments with scientists and researchers, but became frustrated with the caution and slow pace of official groups. She then became involved with grassroots, less scientifically oriented organizations, leading many to disparage her and describe her as lacking objectivity and perhaps being too eager for UFO sightings and contact.

In 1993, Betty developed stomach cancer. Eighty percent of her stomach was removed. In 1995, she wrote and self-published a book, *A Common Sense Approach to UFOs*, recounting her thirty years of UFO research. Betty, a long-term two-pack-a-day smoker, died in 2004 of lung cancer that had metastasized to her brain and adrenal glands.

Debunkers have suggested that Betty confused nightmares with reality and that Barney, through intense empathy, absorbed them. Alternatively, the Hills are described as experiencing a "shared hallucination." Some suggest that what they really saw was Jupiter and Saturn in the night sky. Author and electrical engineer Philip J. Klass, a famous UFO debunker, suggested in his 1966 book, *UFOs Identified*, that what the Hills saw was a "plasma phenomenon" associated with ball lightning.

For more information, see *Captured! The Betty and Barney Hill UFO Experience* by ufologist Stanton T. Friedman and Kathleen Harden, Betty Hill's niece, and *The Betty and Barney Hill Collection*, housed at the

University of New Hampshire, which includes audio-tapes, artwork, films, manuscripts, newspaper clippings, photographs, and personal journals (*www.library.unh. edu/special/index.php/betty-and-barney-hill*).

Holzer, Hans

Hans Holzer was a pioneering paranormal researcher and the world-renowned author of over 140 books dedicated to the occult, extraterrestrials, and other paranormal topics. Born in Vienna on January 26, 1920, Holzer studied archaeology and ancient history at the University of Vienna. Sensing that the political climate was becoming dangerous, the Jewish Holzer family decided that it would be wise to leave Europe and immigrated to the United States, settling in New York City in 1938. Hans studied at Columbia University, earning a Master's degree in comparative religion and, later, a doctorate in parapsychology from the London College of Applied Science. He also taught parapsychology at the New York Institute of Technology.

Holzer's interest in the paranormal began in childhood. He considered himself a scientific investigator of the paranormal and preferred direct communication via a medium to technological attempts to prove the existence of ghosts. He disliked the words "believe" and "disbelieve," saying that one either "knows" or "doesn't know."

Holzer investigated the mystery associated with the Amityville Horror, as well as many other haunted houses. He wrote a non-fiction book, *Murder in Amityville* (1979), which became the basis for the film *Amityville II: The Possession*, as well as two novels, *The Amityville Curse* (1981) and *The Secret of Amityville* (1985). His other books include *Ghosts I've Met* (1965); *ESP and You* (1968); *Hans Holzer's Travel Guide to Haunted Houses* (1998); and *Love beyond the Grave* (1992). He also hosted a television show, *Ghost Hunter*. Hans Holzer died on April 26, 2009.

Home, Daniel Dunglas

Daniel Dunglas Home (pronounced "Hume"), also commonly called Daniel Douglas Home, is widely considered the greatest physical medium. In addition to providing accurate messages from beyond the grave, Home was witnessed elongating his body to impossible lengths in the manner of the comic book superhero Mr. Fantastic. He was able to levitate heavy pieces of furniture—even 100-pound tables. Home manifested rapping sounds, spectral lights, table tipping, and spirits, as well as disembodied ghostly hands that shook hands with his audience.

Although many were and are convinced that Home was a conjuror, the equivalent of a stage magician and hence a charlatan, no one was ever able to prove that he was fraudulent or catch him in a trick, although many tried very hard to do so. Home was extensively studied by experts, investigators, skeptics, and professional debunkers. Unlike most mediums, Home conducted séances and manifested spirits in brightly lit rooms. He never charged for his work, although he did sometimes accept donations. Instead, he lived as a permanent houseguest, with his hosts providing for his needs.

Home considered most other mediums to be frauds. He occasionally worked with other mediums, including Kate Fox, but in general did not socialize with Spiritualists, preferring to mingle with the rich, powerful, and well-connected. His book *Lights and Shadows of Spiritualism*, published in 1877, exposed the tricks used by false mediums.

Home was born March 20, 1833 in the village of Currie, Scotland. His mother, Betsy McNeill Home, came from a highland family famed for psychic prowess. She bore a local reputation as a gifted seer, as did other members of her family. His father, William Home, allegedly the illegitimate son of the tenth Earl of Home, was reportedly a bitter, unhappy man who took his frustrations out on his wife. (The Earls of Home also hold the subsidiary titles Lord Dunglas and Baron Douglas, hence Daniel's middle names.)

The Homes had eight children. Daniel, the third, was so fragile at birth that he was not expected to survive. At the age of one, he was adopted by his mother's childless sister, possibly because, as a sickly child, he needed more care than his harried mother could provide. He may, however, have been given to his aunt because his already powerful psychic abilities were disturbing the household. Even when he was an infant, Daniel's cradle would allegedly rock by itself as if pushed by invisible hands.

By age four, Daniel was exhibiting second sight, describing events occurring far away as if he were an eyewitness. He accurately foretold a cousin's death and later had a vision of his brother Adam's death at sea. Months later, details of Daniel's vision were verified.

In 1842, Daniel moved to Connecticut with his aunt and her husband, joining his parents and siblings who were already there. He was sent to school, where the other children teased him mercilessly. As Daniel was freckled, red-haired, and spoke with a pronounced brogue, his schoolmates nicknamed him Scotchy. Never a strong child, he was unable to participate in sports. After he was diagnosed with tuberculosis, he was quarantined and unable to play with other children at all. Instead, Daniel played alone in the forest or read the Bible. He described himself as surrounded by spirits of the dead.

His paranormal abilities, including clairvoyance, increased. Daniel's sister, Mary Betsey, died at age twelve.

He claimed that her spirit visited him frequently. At thirteen, Daniel received a vision of a childhood friend who had died, fulfilling the vow that the two ailing boys had once made to each other that the first to die would visit the other.

Daniel was fifteen when the Fox sisters came to national attention. By the time he was seventeen, he could produce knocking like the Fox sisters and could also demonstrate telekinesis. He began to attract attention from neighbors, who suspected that he was either possessed by the devil or in league with him. His aunt and uncle, staunch Presbyterians, suspected that Daniel had signed a contract with Satan and consulted ministers, who confirmed their suspicions. (Daniel himself claimed his powers were God's gift.) Daniel was disowned and abruptly ejected from their house. He went to one friend's house, then another's, and would remain essentially a houseguest for the rest of his life.

At Daniel Home's first séance, held in May 1851, a Connecticut newspaper reported that a table moved without being touched and kept moving even when people physically tried to stop it. Daniel was soon much in demand as a medium and began to travel, serving as a medium and spiritual healer.

By 1852, he had begun levitating. Home commonly levitated some five to seven feet off the ground and did it in broad daylight or gaslight, not in dimly lit rooms. In 1868, he levitated out of one window in his friend Lord Adare's London home and then levitated back through another, seventy feet above the ground and before reputable witnesses.

Home journeyed to England in March 1855 and then across Europe, always as the guest of wealthy patrons. Later in 1855, he traveled to Florence, where local peasants considered him a necromancer, able to speak and commune with the dead. Rumors spread that Home fed sacred communion wafers to toads in order to raise evil spirits. (This was once a common accusation against witches. Toads are emblematic of the witch goddess, Hecate.)

On the night of December 5, 1855, Home was ambushed in the street. He was stabbed three times with a dagger, but injured only slightly. His attacker was never charged, and Home soon departed for Paris, where, on February 10, 1856, spirits told him that his powers would leave him for a year—and they did. No reason was ever made public, but for one year, Home was unable to manifest phenomena. He gave no readings, held no séances, and was profoundly depressed. His powers returned exactly a year later in February 1857. His Parisian clientele included Emperor Napoleon III and Princess Eugénie.

Home was eventually arrested in Paris, although whether he was charged with fraud or homosexuality is now unclear. He was released when he threatened to expose a scandal involving homosexuality in the highest echelons of court. (Allegedly, he possessed proof.) Ejected from Paris, he traveled to Russia, where he held séances for Tsar Alexander II. There, he married Alexandrina de Kroll, a seventeen-year-old Russian noblewoman. Author Alexander Dumas, Sr. served as his best man; Count Alexei Tolstoy (author Leo's cousin) acted as a witness.

Alexandrina died of tuberculosis in 1862, and Home found himself in financial straits. They had been married only briefly, and he did not inherit her fortune, which reverted to her family, who did not like him. Home considered a new career and visited the Vatican, seeking to become a sculptor. Within three days, he was accused of being a sorcerer and deported. He then returned to the United States and Britain, becoming a lecturer and offering mediumistic stage exhibitions as well as private séances.

His clientele included authors William Makepeace Thackeray, Sir Edward Bulwer-Lytton, and Ivan Turgenev, as well as artist Dante Gabriel Rossetti, and, most famously, poet and Spiritualist Elizabeth Barrett Browning, who was an ardent fan, although her husband, poet Robert Browning, was not. Browning was not favorably inclined toward Spiritualism or Home, whom he dubbed "Dungball." Browning's poem *Mr. Sludge the Medium*, an almost 2,000-line rant, is believed to have been inspired by Home. It is now suspected that Browning objected to the chummy relationship between his wife and the handsome medium.

More favorably inclined was Robert W. Chambers, author of the classic Gothic horror tale *The King in Yellow*. Initially hostile to Spiritualism, Chambers had a change of heart after attending a séance with Home.

In 1866, Home became embroiled in a scandal when one of his clients, Mrs. Jane Lyons, a rich, seventy-five-year-old London widow, claimed that he had bilked her out of a fortune. According to her, Home had channeled her late husband, who told her that Home was his spiritual son and directed her to provide for his financial needs, offering very specific instructions. She gave Home 12,000 pounds before charging him with fraud.

Home retaliated, claiming that the money had been freely given for his mediumistic services and that she only asked for it back after he rebuffed her sexual advances. The case went to trial, and Home was ordered to return the money. It was a polarizing case, considered very scandalous and embarrassing for all involved. Some friends deserted him—although perhaps more because he hadn't behaved like a gentleman than because of accusations of fraud. Others remained sympathetic, including Chambers, who gave an affidavit on Home's behalf.

In poor health, Home retired in 1873 at thirty-nine. He married for a second time, again to a wealthy Russian noblewoman. He spent the rest of his life traveling the world with his wife and son, Gregoire, and died of tuberculosis in France on June 21, 1886 at fifty-three. He is buried in St-Germain-en-Laye cemetery in Paris.

Hopkins, Budd

Budd Hopkins is a world-renowned abstract expressionist painter and sculptor, and a pioneering ufologist. Born June 15, 1931 in Wheeling, West Virginia, he graduated from Oberlin College in 1953 and moved to New York City. He has resided in New York City and Cape Cod ever since. His work is in the permanent collections of the Metropolitan Museum of Art, the Guggenheim Museum, the Whitney Museum, and the Hirshhorn Museum.

In 1964, together with his wife at that time and a friend, Hopkins witnessed a UFO in broad daylight. Fascinated, he pursued UFO studies, joining the National Investigations Committee on Aerial Phenomena (NICAP). Hopkins has been actively investigating UFOs since 1975. He originally worked alongside hypnotists, but eventually began conducting hypnosis himself. Among the UFO-related books he has authored or coauthored are *Intruders* (1987), *Missing Time* (1988), *Witnessed: The True Story of the Brooklyn Bridge UFO Abductions* (1997), and *Sight Unseen: Science, UFO Invisibility, and Transgenic Beings* (2003). His autobiography, *Art, Life and UFOs*, was published in 2009.

Houdini, Harry

Although actor, author, escape artist, and paranormal investigator Harry Houdini said he was born in Appleton, Wisconsin on April 6, 1874, he wasn't. Instead, he was born Erik Weisz in Budapest on March 24, 1874 to a rabbi and his wife. The family left Hungary for the United States on July 3, 1878. In America, the spelling of his name was changed to Ehrich Weiss. Friends and family called him Ehrie, which evolved into Harry. Houdini, his theatrical name, pays tribute to the French stage magician Robert Houdin.

Harry Houdini was the most renowned and influential stage magician of his time. He is also famous for his quest to discover conclusively whether the dead can communicate with the living. Although sometimes upheld as a paragon by modern skeptics, Houdini was willing to believe in the possibility of life after death, which is why false mediums offended him so greatly.

Early in his career, Houdini faked mediumistic techniques as part of his stage show, as did many other stage magicians. He claimed that his friend, renowned physical medium Ira Davenport, master of the spirit cabinet, revealed professional secrets to him that eventually evolved into Houdini's own fabled escapes. Houdini was a complex person. A Freemason and occult scholar who accrued a sizeable mystical library, he authored several books, including *A Magician Among Spirits*, *The Miracle Mongers: An Exposé*, *On Deception*, and *Houdini On Magic*. For a time, Houdini shared a close friendship with Sir Arthur Conan Doyle, who was a passionate Spiritualist.

Exposing dishonest mediums and charlatans pretending to be mediums became Houdini's obsession. He described himself as the "scourge of spirit mediums," and often attended séances in disguise, frequently with a fake beard. Once he had the tricks and frauds figured out, he would snatch off his disguise, proclaiming: "I am Houdini! You are a fraud!"

Houdini was extremely close to his mother, Cecelia Steiner Weiss. When she died in 1913, he attempted to contact her via mediumistic means. Doyle's wife sometimes gave readings via automatic writing, and together they attempted to contact Cecelia. Doyle and his wife fervently believed that the communication they received was real, but Houdini rejected it.

The written message Doyle's wife gave Houdini began with a drawing of a cross, a symbol that Mrs. Weiss, the wife of a rabbi, would never have used. It was also given in English, a language she could neither speak nor write. Mediums commonly deliver messages in languages that they themselves cannot understand, whether orally or in writing. As Houdini knew, if truly entranced, there is no reason that Mrs. Doyle should not have been able to deliver a message in Hungarian, Mrs. Weiss' primary language, or in any other. Doyle later claimed that the cross was not actually part of the message, but rather was how Mrs. Doyle began all her automatic writing sessions, as she felt that this would prevent negative spirits from manifesting. The friendship between Houdini and Doyle, however, never recovered from this disappointing episode.

Houdini made compacts with approximately one dozen people, agreeing to communicate with each of them after death and creating an elaborate code, including secret handshakes, to prove the communiqués were genuine. He complained that no one ever returned to him. He attended séances in which the medium claimed to bring up the spirits he requested, but, according to Houdini, the agreed-upon signals were never correct.

Houdini died on October 31, 1926. He had given his wife and former theatrical partner, Bess, instructions for contacting him after death. They had agreed on a secret message to be delivered in their own secret code. After his death, Bess promised a $10,000 reward to anyone who could deliver that message. Three years after Houdini's death, Lily Dale medium Arthur Ford (1897–1971) gave Bess what he claimed was the correct message: "Rosabelle, believe." It was delivered in the complex code that Bess and Harry had used in a vaudeville act years before.

Bess wrote a statement acknowledging that Ford's message was delivered in their secret code and was, she believed, genuinely from Houdini. Two newspaper reporters covered this event. One reporter later accused Ford of fraud, saying that he had told her the story on the night previous to the event so that she could have the newspaper story ready for a deadline. Some asked why she had then reported a story that she knew to be suspicious or false. There had been rumors of romance between Bess and Ford. Accused of conspiring with the medium, Bess retracted her statement and insisted until her death that Houdini had never communicated with her from beyond the grave. To this day, every year on Halloween, the anniversary of his death, many hold séances to communicate with Houdini.

The Plaza Hotel and Casino stands on the site of the first train depot in Las Vegas, which was built in 1905 and demolished in 1970. It is allegedly haunted by a ghost. Some say it is the ghost of a stagehand who committed suicide, but others insist that the ghost is Houdini. In either case, the Plaza's ghost is a prankster who enjoys playing tricks with people's belongings.

Jürgenson, Friedrich

Considered the father and foremost pioneer of Electronic Voice Phenomena (EVP), Friedrich Jürgenson was a renaissance man who spoke ten languages. An archaeologist, painter, and opera singer, he was as skilled with technology as with fine art, working as a recording artist and a documentary filmmaker.

Friedrich was born in Odessa on February 8, 1903 to a family of Swedish and Danish descent. Trapped by the Russian revolution, his family was permitted to leave the Soviet Union in 1925 and move to Estonia, where Friedrich trained as a painter, singer, and musician. Friedrich studied in Berlin, where his tutor was Jewish bass singer, Tito Scipa. In 1932, Scipa fled the Nazis, traveling to Palestine. Friedrich accompanied him, remaining there for six years. A promising career as an opera singer was anticipated for him. He continued his studies in Milan in 1938.

In 1943, Friedrich suffered voice damage and began to focus on a career as a painter, moving to Sweden. Employed by the Vatican to catalogue their archaeological works, Friedrich painted four portraits of Pope Pius XII and later three of Pope Paul VI. The Vatican provided him with full access to Pompeii, and his first major art exhibition was held among its ruins.

In 1957, Friedrich purchased an early portable tape recorder. On June 12, 1959, he brought his tape recorder to his Swedish country house intending to record wild-bird songs. Later, while replaying his tapes, he heard garbled human voices, although he was sure that he had been completely alone at the time of taping. The voices he heard are described as resembling those of the Daleks in the British television series *Dr Who*. Intrigued, Jürgenson continued to investigate.

He began making recordings of nothing. On tapes that should have revealed utter silence, he consistently detected voices. Jürgenson made thousands of these recordings. Although many of the voices were unfamiliar to him, he recognized others, including that of his deceased mother, who called him by his pet name, Friedel. He realized that his recordings were capturing the voices of the dead and that technology could facilitate communication between the dead and the living. In addition to the voices of family and friends, Jürgenson was also able to identify the voice of Van Gogh.

In 1960, a voice directed him to substitute a radio for his tape recorder. The radio became his primary mode of communicating with what he described as his friends from the other side. He originally set the radio dial between frequencies, but eventually fixed the receiving frequencies between 1,445 and 1,500 kHz. 1,485.0 kHz is now known as the Jürgenson frequency in his honor. Jürgenson predicted that messages from beyond would eventually be received via television as well.

In 1964, Jürgenson published a book, *Voices from Space*. At the time of publication, he held a press conference in which his rational, scientific manner attracted favorable attention. Various paranormal societies made contact with him. Jürgenson's other books include *Radio Link with the Dead* and *Radio and Microphone Contact with the Dead*. He continued to lecture and hoped to found a paranormal research society in Italy. Friedrich Jürgenson died in October 1987, leaving hundreds of tape recordings. Some have been released on a CD: *Friedrich Jürgenson: From the Studio for Audioscopic Research* (Ash International).

Levitation

Levitation is the art of defying the law of gravity. It involves raising physical objects into the air without visible means. People possessing telekinetic powers are said to be able to lift objects with their minds and move them or have them hover in the air. These objects may be as light as a pencil or as massive as pianos. People and other living beings may also levitate.

Levitation is among the feats associated with physical mediumship. During séances, tables may levitate or the mediums themselves may levitate with assistance from spirits. The most famous incident involved medium Daniel Dunglas Home during a séance in December 1868 in London. Home fell into a trance, floated out one third-floor window, and then floated back inside through

another window. This was accomplished in the presence of witnesses perceived as irreproachable. Skeptics insist that the witnesses were hypnotized or shared some sort of mass hallucination. Various theories exist to explain how Home accomplished his feat, but so far no one has used any of them to replicate it.

Levitation is not limited to Spiritualism. It is also considered a sacred art associated with saints and holy people. Joseph of Cupertino, the patron saint of astronauts and pilots, is known as "the flying saint" and "the flying friar" because of his many feats of levitation. Advanced practitioners of Transcendental Meditation claim to have mastered levitation under the training of Maharishi Mahesh Yogi.

Lily Dale

Sixty miles south of Buffalo, New York is Lily Dale, the largest Spiritualist community on Earth. It is also the oldest Spiritualist community in the United States and, most probably, in the world. The village of Lily Dale was established on the shores of Lake Cassadaga in 1879 as a summer camp for Spiritualists. At one time, there may have been as many as sixteen Spiritualist summer camps throughout the United States. In addition to Lily Dale, only a few now survive, including Indiana's Camp Chesterfield, Wisconsin's Camp Wonewoc, and Cassadaga Spiritualist Camp in Central Florida.

Lily Dale evolved into and remains a Spiritualist mecca. Originally nicknamed the City of Light because it was among the first regions of New York State to have electricity, the moniker eventually came to imply inner light. Many of the most prominent mediums were in residence in Lily Dale at one time or another, including the Bangs sisters and the Campbell brothers.

Thousands visit Lily Dale every summer during its annual tourist season, which runs from late June until the last Sunday of August. An extensive schedule of lectures, workshops, and other activities featuring renowned authors, Spiritualist leaders, and paranormal researchers is available. Healing services are offered, as are demonstrations of mediumship. Hotels sell out quickly and must be booked well in advance. Accommodations are also available in guest houses and campgrounds.

Lily Dale can be extremely cold in the winter, which is why summer is its high season. However, Lily Dale is a year-round residential community of Spiritualist teachers and mediums. An increasing number of activities are available off-season as well.

The residents of Lily Dale are spiritually dynamic, but the very land is also considered to emanate tremendous mystical power. According to legend, Lily Dale was built over a site held sacred by local Native Americans. Many mediums suggest that the veil between realms is especially sheer in Lily Dale, thus facilitating psychic activity and mediumship. Many claim to have witnessed fairies and elemental spirits in Lily Dale's forests.

The Lily Dale Museum, housed in a one-room 1890 schoolhouse, displays items from the Fox family, including their family bible. In April 1916, the Foxes' Hydesville cottage was dismantled and relocated to Lily Dale, where it was destroyed by fire in 1955. The peddler's pack found behind the false partition was rescued from the fire and remains on display in the Lily Dale Museum. The museum also houses an extensive collection of Spiritualist magazines, newspapers, and pamphlets, as well as precipitated spirit paintings.

Lincoln's Ghost

The ghost of the sixteenth president of the United States, Abraham Lincoln (1809–1865), allegedly haunts the White House. Sometimes just called "the White House ghost," Lincoln's ghost knocks on doors and roams through the halls, moving restlessly from room to room. He wears a tormented look on his face and a plaid shawl over his shoulders.

Among those claiming to have seen Lincoln's ghost are fellow presidents Theodore Roosevelt and Harry Truman, as well as numerous members of the White House staff. President John F. Kennedy asked Lincoln for advice on matters of importance. First Lady Eleanor Roosevelt used Lincoln's bedroom as her study. Although she never claimed to have actually seen the ghost, she described a sensation of being watched while in that room that she credited to his presence.

President Ronald Reagan's daughter, Maureen, and her husband claimed to have seen the ghost on multiple occasions in the Lincoln bedroom. She described it as a "transparent figure." Reagan's dog would allegedly stand outside the Lincoln bedroom and bark, but refuse to enter.

Perhaps the most dramatic story involving Lincoln's ghost concerns Winston Churchill, who stayed in the White House during World War II. Having just emerged from the bath, he walked naked into the adjoining bedroom where he saw Lincoln standing beside the fireplace. Recognizing the former president and maintaining his cool, Churchill said: "Good evening, Mr. President. You seem to have me at a disadvantage." The ghost smiled and vanished.

Abraham Lincoln was no stranger to psychic phenomena while alive. He experienced visions, a paranormal gift he attributed to his psychic mother, Nancy Hanks Lincoln, who died when Lincoln was nine. He claimed to have dreamed his own death twice, most famously in April 1865 when he dreamt that he was lying in bed listening to the sound of weeping. In his dream, he got up and followed the sound into the East Room of the White House, where he saw a line of people paying their respects to a body lying in state guarded by

four soldiers. The corpse's face was covered. Lincoln, in his dream, asked one of the soldiers who had died. The soldier responded that it was the president who had been killed by an assassin. Lincoln told his wife and several friends of this dream. Later that same month, Abraham Lincoln was shot and killed by actor John Wilkes Booth.

Lincoln and his wife, Mary Todd Lincoln, lost three of their four sons. Following the 1862 death of Willie, Mary, hoping to communicate with her dead boys, became fascinated with séances. Lincoln read books written by Spiritualists. He was discreet in public and his beliefs remain unclear, but Mary openly embraced Spiritualism, attending séances in mediums' homes. At least eight séances were held in the White House during the Lincoln administration. It is believed that Lincoln attended at least one. After his assassination, several Spiritualists visited Mary in the White House. Later in life, she attended séances under assumed names in an attempt to test mediums and determine which were legitimate and which fake.

Lincoln's ghost is particularly active and is not confined to the White House. It has also been seen near his Springfield, Illinois tomb, as well as on the balcony of Ford's Theater in the company of the ghost of Booth, his murderer. Rumor has it that the ghosts are attempting to settle their differences.

Lincoln's ghost has also been reported at the Parker House, across the street from Ford's, where he was taken after being shot and where he died. There are also annual sightings of the apparition of his funeral train on the anniversary of its journey. Some actually see the ghost train, while others hear its whistle.

Medium

A medium is a conduit or bridge—a person possessing the capacity to facilitate communication between humans and spirits. Modern Spiritualist mediums typically deliver messages from those no longer among the living. This concept is not new, but ancient—although mediums have been known by other names, for example, oracle or sibyl. The most famous medium of all may be the Bible's Woman of Endor, also sometimes called the Medium of Endor or the Witch of Endor. Although mediums are now most closely identified with Spiritualism, not all mediums are Spiritualists: mediums may derive from any spiritual tradition or practice any religion.

There are different types of mediums, and they can manifest psychic skills in many ways. They may demonstrate clairaudience, clairvoyance, or clairsentience. Some use spirit boards or automatic writing to commune with the spirit world. Those who created precipitated spirit paintings were also considered mediums, as are spirit photographers. Some mediums may channel spirits, essentially becoming a portal for them. Spirits may speak directly through the voice of a medium.

Some mediums produce nothing but messages. This is the hardest type of mediumship to fake. Messages will either resonate or not. Predictions will either prove true or not. Modern Spiritualism classifies this type of medium as a *message medium*.

Some mediums allegedly channel phenomena that are caused by spirits. Some may attract or generate certain types of spirit-derived phenomena. These are classified by modern Spiritualism as *physical mediums*.

Phenomena produced by physical mediums include rapping and knocking noises, levitation, table tipping, spirit materializations, apports, and ectoplasm. The more theatrical physical mediumship becomes, the easier it is to fake. Many stage magicians produce similar phenomena for entertainment purposes. Some of the earliest celebrity stage magicians produced shows that resembled séances. A stage magician's cabinet is not unlike a medium's spirit cabinet. One catalog, *Gambols with the Ghosts*, published in Chicago in 1901 by Ralph E. Sylvestre & Company, advertised "Spiritualistic effects," including equipment for ghost materializations, slate writing, self-playing musical instruments, and self-rapping tables.

Following the 1848 events in the Fox family's Hydesville cottage, Spiritualism evolved into a stylish fad. Mediums and their investigators achieved celebrity status. People attended séances to be thrilled, amazed, and entertained. As audiences increased, there was greater demand for special effects. This pressure may have encouraged even genuine mediums to

enhance their séances through fraud. In the 1940s, the Spiritualist community of Lily Dale outlawed physical mediumship in favor of exclusively message mediumship except in classes or within private circles.

Someone may honestly, consistently, and always display true mediumship. On the other hand, someone may be completely and consistently fraudulent. These people, however, are *not* mediums, but charlatans. If they are fraudulent, then they are not fraudulent mediums, but only impersonators, in the same way that someone who pretends to be a medical doctor is not actually a physician.

True mediumistic talent cannot always be produced on demand. The spirits are not always cooperative. Not every medium is able to turn his or her talent on or off at will. A medium is not a stage magician. He or she may not be able to produce an impressive apport at every séance. Thus sometimes, genuine mediums, feeling pressured to produce, may occasionally resort to fraudulent behavior. Likewise, someone who initially begins as a fraud may, in the process of defrauding, discover, perhaps to their own surprise, that they possess true mediumistic skill.

Men in Black

People who have encountered what they believe to be extraterrestrials often claim later to have been visited by men dressed in black suits whose goal is to persuade

 them not to discuss their encounters with others. These men wear impenetrable black sunglasses and drive nondescript black cars. They are humorless, emotionless, and aggressive, and usually know a lot about those they visit—as if the person were under surveillance. These men in black may display government identification, but later attempts to locate or contact them tend to hit dead ends. It is possible that not all men in black match this description. Witnesses to the Roswell incident described being threatened and intimidated by government agents who did not dress as stereotypical men in black.

Are the men in black really government agents? Some think they are actually extraterrestrials, or possibly androids controlled by extraterrestrials. The phenomenon of men in black was first reported in the 1950s. They are now easily identifiable staples of paranormal entertainment. Legends of men in black inspired the comic book series, *Men in Black*, which, in turn, served as inspiration for the 1997 hit movie starring Will Smith and Tommie Lee Jones, as well as its cleverly titled 2002 sequel, *Men in Black II*.

Mirror Writing

Also known as mirror script, mirror writing is created by writing "backward"—that is, by reversing the direction in which a language is usually written. Words written in this way appear backward when looked at directly, but are read correctly when displayed in a mirror. The easiest way to read mirror writing is to hold it up to a mirror. A common, mundane example is the word "ambulance," which is typically written in mirror/reverse text on the front of those vehicles so that drivers glancing in their rearview mirrors will instantly recognize the word and get out of the way.

The ability to create mirror writing naturally and effortlessly may be genetic, and is possibly a form of dyslexia. The most famous practitioner of mirror writing was Leonardo Da Vinci. His notes on his image *The Vitruvian Man* appear in mirror writing, for example.

Mirror writing can also be used as code and can serve as a form of physical mediumship. Some mediums produce automatic mirror writing while entranced, although they are unable to do so at other times. Kate Fox was among the medium practitioners of mirror writing. During the 18th and 19th centuries, mirror writing was popular in the Ottoman Empire, where it was perceived as having mystical significance.

Missing Time

Being abducted and taken aboard an alien spacecraft should be a memorable experience, and yet many self-identified abductees initially have gaps in their memories known as *missing time*. These individuals suffer amnesia about a specific period and are unable to recall experiences, where they were, and what they did or witnessed. For example, they may remember driving down a road and then recall getting back into the car. What happened in the interim is lost. They cannot recall how, why, or when they left the car, thereby necessitating the return.

In general, these memories can be recalled via hypnosis, but sometimes they begin to seep back even without treatment—although not necessarily in a coherent fashion. Under hypnosis, however, abductees may be able to recall experiences in vivid and minute detail. Missing time is considered a form of post-traumatic amnesia and may occur in response to any highly stressful experience. For more information, see *Missing Time* by Budd Hopkins (Ballantine Books, 1988).

Near-Death Experiences (NDE)

To be at death's doorstep—and to survive—can be a life-changing experience. The term Near-Death Experience (NDE)—sometimes called Pre-Death Experience—refers to the accounts of those who almost

died, but then lived to describe what they experienced. A surprising number of people give similar descriptions of these events. Many tell of an intense awareness or even just a sense of an otherworld, an afterlife. Some describe otherworldly beings like angels or ancestors who arrived to protect them. In some cases, these otherworldly beings urge the dying person back to the realm of the living. An estimated fifteen million Americans and possibly 5 percent of the total global population have had an NDE.

Omm Sety

Dorothy Louise Eady, the future Omm Sety (sometimes spelled Seti), was born in London on January 16, 1904. At the age of three, she fell down a flight of stairs and was knocked unconscious. The family physician examined her and, finding no signs of life, left to file a coroner's report. By the time he returned an hour later, the little girl was jumping on her bed and appeared to have made a full recovery. Her parents, however, were distressed. Dorothy, upon awakening, had demanded to "go home" and continued to make that demand. She *was* home. What could she mean?

Dorothy began having recurrent dreams of herself as a temple priestess. Her dreams were extremely detailed: she could actually see the temple in which she had served. When Dorothy was four, her parents took her to visit London's British Museum. As she later recalled, when she stepped into the Egyptian galleries, she immediately realized that she was "home." She ran around the galleries kissing the feet of statues, much to her parents' embarrassment, and had to be forcibly removed when it was time to leave. Her obsession with ancient Egypt grew. Three years later, when Dorothy read an illustrated article, *The Temple of Sety the First at Abydos,* she recognized the temple of her dreams, but was perplexed as to why the photos showed the temple in ruins and lacking its beautiful gardens.

Dorothy began to immerse herself in Egyptology. She studied with Sir Ernest A. Wallis Budge, Keeper of Antiquities at the British Museum, who taught her to decipher hieroglyphs. Memories of her past life in ancient Egypt returned via vivid dreams, automatic writing, and conversations with her beloved, Pharaoh Sety I.

She claimed that, during Sety I's reign, she had been a fourteen-year-old priestess named Bentreshyt who had lived at the Abydos temple complex under a vow of chastity. Bentreshyt had participated in the annual passion plays dedicated to the deity Osiris that reenacted his life, death, and resurrection. Sety I encountered Bentreshyt at the temple, fell in love with her, and seduced her. She conceived a child and was brutally punished, dying without

implicating Sety, as her interrogators desired. The pharaoh was broken-hearted. His soul had longed for hers ever since, and he had attempted to make contact with her lifetime after lifetime. Now he finally had, or so Dorothy claimed.

Dorothy eventually married an Egyptian student in London. When he returned to Egypt in 1933, she went with him. Dorothy was twenty-nine at the time and never left Egypt again. She bore one son, whom she insisted on naming Sety after the pharaoh much to the annoyance of her fairly secular, but conventional, Muslim husband. In Egyptian tradition, women become known as the mother of their first son. Thus Dorothy became Omm Sety, literally "Mother of Sety," the name she would bear ever after.

The marriage did not last. Dorothy's eccentricities did not endear her to her husband's family. After the couple divorced, Dorothy became the first female employee of the Egyptian Antiquities Department. She worked with the finest Egyptologists and archaeologists and became friends with many. In 1958, she bought a one-way ticket to Abydos, once Egypt's sacred religious center, but then just ruins in the desert. Omm Sety was largely responsible for restoring Abydos' reputation as a holy city.

For the rest of her life, Dorothy lived like a peasant with no electricity or running water. She created a daily religious calendar for herself and practiced traditional Egyptian religion within the old ruined shrines. She became a tourist attraction herself, serving as a volunteer tour guide in Abydos. Eventually, people made the trek into the desert just to meet this eccentric Englishwoman. The spirit of Sety I found a way to visit her there, and they resumed their love affair. With her permission, he was able to manifest himself by drawing on her life force. She consulted him on matters of Egyptology.

Much that Omm Sety claimed was told to her by Pharaoh Sety has proven true. Various archaeological discoveries were made based on information she received from Sety I and passed on to her friends in the Egyptian Antiquities Department. Many archaeologists and Egyptologists secretly consulted Omm Sety. They were afraid that association with this eccentric woman would taint their reputations, yet she proved consistently to be a font of accurate information. Some things Sety told her have yet to be proven. She claimed that the Great Sphinx is older than is now generally believed and was intended to honor the Egyptian deity Lord Horus.

On April 21, 1981, Omm Sety died in her sleep in her cottage in Abydos, surrounded by her beloved cats. Neighbors found her body when they heard the cats crying. She is buried in Abydos between the Sety and Ramses temples. For more information, see Jonathan Cott's *The Search for Omm Sety* (Grand Central Publishing, 1989); *Omm Sety's Egypt: A Story of Ancient Mysteries, Secret Lives, and The Lost History of the Pharaohs* by Hanny el Zeini and Catherine Dees (St. Lynn's Press, 2007). In 1981, the BBC made a film, *Omm Sety and Her Egypt.*

Parapsychology

Parapsychology is a modern discipline that explores the existence of psychic powers and certain other paranormal topics using scientific method. Invention of the word is generally credited to German philosopher Max Dessoir (1867–1947) in approximately 1889. By the 1930s, the word had become increasingly popular as a substitute for what was once known as *psychical research*, which possessed too much of an occult tinge for many scientific researchers.

Parapsychology is not the study of everything paranormal. Cryptozoology, for example, is a completely distinct branch of paranormal studies. Instead, parapsychology focuses on paranormal phenomena associated with humans. Its goal is to discover irrefutable scientific evidence of paranormal psychological processes, including mind-matter interactions like telekinesis, the ability to move objects without actually touching them, and extrasensory perceptions like telepathy or clairvoyance. Parapsychologists also study the possibility of communication between the living and the dead, human survival after death, and reincarnation. Thus phone calls from the dead fall under the category of parapsychology, but chupacabras do not. Many parapsychologists believe that it will eventually be possible to prove the truth or falsehood of the many topics that fall under its broad umbrella conclusively and scientifically.

Phone Calls
from the Dead

On Mrs. Smith's wedding anniversary, her phone rang. When she answered it, her husband was on the line, telling her a little personal joke that only the two of them shared. Sounds ordinary enough—except that her husband was dead.

A young man is desperately in trouble. While pondering his options, his phone rings. When he answers it, his caller immediately, without being prompted, offers comfort and excellent advice. The name by which this caller identifies herself sounds vaguely familiar. Later, the young man describes this mysterious phone call to older relatives who recognize the name as a family member who had passed on several years before.

These are examples of phone calls from the dead—calls received from those who are irrefutably deceased. (If the person on the line reveals that they have faked their death and are still alive, that phone call, by definition, is not from the dead.) Phone calls from the dead are considered a form of Electronic Voice Phenomena (EVP). How these phone calls are accomplished remains a mystery.

In general, phone calls from the dead are received by ordinary people who do not necessarily demonstrate any particular psychic talents. In general, the

content of these calls is ordinary, if sometimes important. The dead may be calling to offer comfort or advice, or reveal where money is hidden. They are not calling to reveal secrets of the afterlife—or, if they are, those calls are not being reported.

The simplest phone calls from the dead are brief and one-sided. The caller does not engage in conversation or respond to questions. The caller says whatever he or she has to say, sometimes repeatedly, and then there will be silence until the person receiving the call breaks the connection by hanging up. It is rare for this type of dead caller to terminate the call.

More complex, prolonged conversations are rare—or at least, rarely reported—and usually involve two-way conversation. Typically, the receiver of the call is unaware at the time that the caller is dead, only learning this later. The caller usually avoids all conversation that could lead to this revelation—answering other questions, for instance, but ignoring requests to make future plans.

Phone calls from the living to the dead have also been reported. The living person, unaware that the person being called has died, dials the person's telephone number *and the person picks up!* They have a perfectly normal conversation, and it is only after the call ends that the caller learns that the other person was already dead at the time. For more information, see *Phone Calls from the Dead* by D. Scott Rogo and Raymond Bayless (Berkley Books, 1979).

Poltergeist

Something invisible pinches your arm. If it is only your imagination, why does a black-and-blue mark appear? Did those books spontaneously fall off the shelf and onto your head, or did they have a little help from an invisible hand? You're sleeping alone, so who pulled the blankets off? And those noises in the night—are they really just the sound of the house "settling"? What else could they be?

Poltergeist is a German word that literally means "knocking ghost" or "knocking spirit." The word first appeared in English in the mid 19th century. Much controversy remains, however, regarding the true nature of these beings. Is a poltergeist a type of ghost possessing consciousness and intelligence, or merely the manifestation of excess psychic energy? In other words, is someone in the house exuding so much psychic energy that, unknowingly, they are causing strange, paranormal phenomena to occur? Poltergeists often manifest in proximity to adolescents, especially young girls. It is possible that psychic energy develops in a manner similar to hormones and needs time to stabilize and balance. Another theory suggests that certain types of spirits, attracted to this excess energy, actually create the paranormal phenomena. Poltergeists tend to be eerie and unpleasant. Poltergeist activity ranges from the strange and mildly disturbing to the downright dangerous.

Precipitated Spirit Paintings

Also known as precipitated spirit portraits and precipitated spirit art, these portraits of the deceased were produced by spirits facilitated by human mediums, but without the use of human hands. In other words, precipitated paintings were created by artists who did not actually touch the canvas. Spirits did more than just guide the medium's hands, however, as with automatic painting. In precipitated spirit paintings, spirits actually produced the images. A precipitated spirit portrait just manifested.

Precipitated spirit paintings tend to be large, even life-size, portraits of someone who is no longer living at the time the portrait is made, although other types do exist. In most, the subject's eyes gaze out at the viewer. The first recorded demonstration of this phenomenon was by the Bangs sisters in 1894. Many Spiritualists consider the Bangs sisters and the Campbell brothers to have been the foremost practitioners and masters of this form of mediumship. Although no one is currently creating new precipitated spirit portraits—or at least not bringing them to public attention—the surviving examples remain among the most intriguing and mysterious of the paranormal arts, subject to intense study by researchers.

The process of creating a precipitated spirit portrait was considered a type of séance. A blank, clean canvas or paper was stretched over a wooden frame by the medium. A pot of oil paint was usually present, but no paintbrushes were permitted in the room. Since human hands allegedly did not create these paintings, no brushes were necessary. Present in the room was the medium who facilitated the process, the person requesting the portrait (known as a "sitter"), and possibly other observers. All participants may have rested their hands or fingers on the canvas in the same manner that hands are rested on a spirit board.

The sitter mentally focused on the deceased person they wished to contact, whose identity may or may not have been revealed to the medium. Since spirits hypothetically created the image, it was not important for the medium to know the identity or appearance of the subject of the hoped-for portrait. The precipitated portrait gradually began to appear on the canvas or paper, in a manner similar to the gradual development of a Polaroid picture. It usually took between fifteen minutes to an hour for the image to appear fully.

Needless to say, precipitated spirit portraits were *extremely* controversial. Were the mediums who created them avaricious hoaxers intent on exploiting the grieving, or were they sincere Spiritualists who sought only to comfort the living and prove the continuity of life? Can spirits create portraits? Were paintings created in advance and canvases switched using sleight of hand?

Although many assume that precipitated spirit portraits *must* have been fakes, it wasn't that easy to fake them. In most of the existing cases, although not all, no prior photograph of the subject existed. Often, clients desired precipitated spirit portraits specifically because they lacked photographs of loved ones and wished to retain an image. Although lights may have been dimmed, rooms in which the paintings were created were never completely dark. All eyes—and sometimes hands—were inevitably on the canvas.

Whether or not these portraits were crafted by spirits, they are unusual works of art that confound art experts, who have been unable to determine what medium was used in their creation. Although a pot of oil paints was usually present during the séance, precipitated spirit portraits resemble pastels, or modern airbrush paintings. They closely resemble color photographs, but the most famous of them were created before color photography existed. (Commercial color film was not available until 1907.) In general, no brushstrokes are visible. Spirit portraits often display a powdery texture described as resembling the powder on butterfly wings. Images sometimes appear to be embedded in the canvas.

Many precipitated spirit portraits radiate a magical quality. Sometimes eyes that first appear closed spontaneously open later. Because most famous precipitated spirit portraits are hauntingly beautiful, many people are captivated and fascinated by them as works of art, whether or not they accept them as authentic spirit paintings. There are precipitated spirit paintings in the collection of the Lily Dale Museum, as well as at Camp Chesterfield, Indiana. Because these portraits were created for individuals, many most likely remain in private collections.

The most famous precipitated spirit portrait preceded modern Spiritualism by centuries. In the mid 16th century, the image of Mexico's Lady of Guadalupe miraculously appeared on an agave-fiber *tilma*, a type of indigenous cloak, belonging to a man named Juan Diego. The Vatican has confirmed the authenticity of this miracle.

Scientific analysis indicates that there was some embellishment of the image on the tilma, but the main portion of the image cannot be explained satisfactorily. No signs of human creation appear to exist. The blue pigment used cannot be identified or reproduced. Furthermore, an agave-fiber tilma should have a life expectancy of approximately a decade before it disintegrates. Yet the cloak with its image survives and is currently on display in the Basilica of Guadalupe in Mexico City. For more information, see Ron Nagy's *Precipitated Spirit Paintings* (Galde Press, 2006), which includes reproductions of many precipitated portraits by the Bangs sisters and Campbell brothers. Nagy also discusses interesting findings regarding images found within the eyes on some paintings.

Precognition

You have a vividly detailed dream of a future plane crash. You see exactly when and where the crash will occur, as well as the airline involved. Three days later, exactly such a crash occurs. You have experienced precognition.

Precognition—the ability to foretell the future, to know what will happen before it occurs—is the most frequently reported form of extrasensory perception. The word literally means "to know before" and is defined as direct knowledge of the future derived by extrasensory means. Its complementary power is *retrocognition*, the capacity to know past events psychically that could not be known otherwise.

Not everyone experiences precognition in the same way. Although some experience it in dreams, others have waking visions. Sometimes, precognition is highly detailed and accurate, but it may also be vague and hazy. You know there will be a plane crash, but you don't know precisely when and where. Those who learn how to control, harness, and refine this innate ability to foretell the future may become prophets, oracles, professional psychics, or fortune-tellers.

Premonitions

Sometimes, you have a bad or good feeling about something about to happen. That's a premonition. A premonition is more than a hunch—it is a powerful, sometimes overwhelming, feeling of impending doom or good fortune.

Premonitions and precognition are similar, but not identical. With precognition, someone dreams or otherwise "knows" that there will be a plane crash very soon. Depending on the precognition, this knowledge may or may not be extremely detailed. A clairvoyant or someone possessing second sight may actually "see" this future event, including the name of the airline written on the body of the plane.

A premonition is hazier. Someone about to board a plane has a bad feeling about it and abruptly changes his or her plans. The individual does not envision the crash, but merely knows that he or she does not want to be on that plane. That person has experienced a premonition.

Not all premonitions are negative. Someone may rarely play the lottery, but, acting on a premonition that today is a lucky day, purchases a winning ticket. In general, premonitions cannot be controlled. A person is a passive recipient of a premonition, but must then decide whether or not to act on it.

Price, Harry

Considered by many to be the original ghost hunter, Harry Price, born in London in 1881, transformed ghost research from an elitist hobby into a popular interest. Price's father was a grocer and traveling salesman. In 1889, Harry saw a performance by a stage magician and was instantly spellbound. He became an amateur magician and began amassing an immense library of books about magic. When he was fifteen, Harry and a friend spent the night in an allegedly haunted house, the first of many ghost investigations. In 1908, Price married Constance Mary Knight, a wealthy heiress, and was able to devote himself entirely to the ghost hunting and paranormal research he loved.

An inventor, skilled with practical electronics and mechanics, Price invented his own ghost-hunting and medium-testing devices. A theatrical, flamboyant man, he was an excellent conjurer and thus possessed a sharp eye for sleight of hand. Price was responsible for exposing a number of charlatans. A debunker who was simultaneously open to the possibility of authentic paranormal events, Price eventually became more interested in exploring genuine psychic phenomena, rather than merely debunking frauds. This led some of Price's fellow psychic researchers to scorn him for accepting that some mediums might be genuine. There may also have been an element of class snobbery involved. Most of Price's fellow researchers came from elegant backgrounds, while he was a grocer's son. Many resented his lack of scientific training and university degree, as well as his background in conjuring, and treated him with open contempt.

Price joined the Society for Psychical Research (SPR) in 1920. In 1923, he founded the National Laboratory for Psychical Research located in the London Spiritualist Alliance. The SPR strongly disapproved of this close association with Spiritualism, considering that it interfered with scientific objectivity. In 1927, the SPR returned Price's massive book collection, which he had given them as a gift. He remained a member of the SPR until his death, although he was not always welcome there. He was also a member of the Ghost Club.

In the 1930s, Price became world famous as a psychical researcher. He is the author of the book *Fifty Years of Psychical Research*. Price died at home of a heart attack on March 29, 1948 at sixty-seven. Following his death, allegations of fraud were made against him, but none were proven.

Project Blue Book

Between 1947 and 1969, the United States Air Force investigated UFOs. These investigations, officially begun on June 30, 1947, evolved into Project Sign, which was formally initiated on January 26, 1948. On February 12, 1949, the name was changed to Project Grudge, which then evolved into Project Blue Book on March 25, 1952. Although superficially this may appear to be a continuous investigation punctuated by name changes, these projects were subject to changes in Air Force priorities and internal politics. Many use the name Project Blue Book to refer to all of the Air Force's official UFO research.

Project Blue Book had two official goals. The first was to determine whether UFOs were a threat to national security; the second was to analyze the vast quantity of UFO-related data. According to Project Blue Book's official findings, no evidence indicates that UFOs are of extraterrestrial origin. No UFO reported, investigated, and evaluated by the Air Force was demonstrated to be a threat to American national security. No evidence discovered by the Air Force or submitted to them represents technological developments beyond modern science.

Project Blue Book Special Report 14, the largest study completed by the U.S. Air Force, analyzed approximately 3,200 alleged UFO sightings. Twenty-one percent of these sightings remain unexplained.

Another 9.5 percent are listed as having insufficient evidence to explain. The Project Blue Book Archive (*www.projectbluebookarchive.org*) provides free access to over 50,000 U.S. government documents pertaining to UFOs.

Psionics

Psionic is a word invented in the 20th century as an umbrella term to describe human paranormal behavior. It refers to all powers of the mind—from the passive (telepathy or clairvoyance) to the active (telekinesis or pyrokinesis). Psionics is the study of all these powers.

In 1942, the root word *psi* was proposed as a general term to encompass extrasensory perception and telekinesis, considered passive psi and active psi respectively. This was later modified to *psionic*, merging the words *psi* with *electronics*, implicitly implying that the paranormal workings of the mind could be made to function as consistently and reliably as a machine.

Psychomanteum

A *psychomanteum*, also spelled *psychomantium*, is a small mirrored room or cabinet that facilitates communication with spirits. Also known as an apparition booth, the structure encourages spirits to become visible in a mirror. It is a smaller, more intimate version of a carnival's House of Mirrors, but without trick mirrored panels that create distorted images. A psychomanteum can also be compared to a mirrored spirit cabinet. Candles or low-wattage lightbulbs can be used to further facilitate the process. Psychomanteums were popular during the heyday of Spiritualism.

The name derives from ancient Greek oracular shrines dedicated to Hades and other deities where the living could contact and consult the deceased. These shrines, the original psychomanteums, did not feature mirrors, but were typically small underground chambers. The modern mirrored version derives from the ancient method of divination known as "scrying." Scrying involves gazing into a flat, reflective surface until a trance state is achieved. The most ancient form of scrying involves gazing at the waters of a still, peaceful lake. Traditional scrying devices include pans of water and ink, as well as crystal balls and mirrors. The modern psychomanteum expands the concept of mirror gazing.

Psychometry

Psychometry is the psychic ability to receive information through touch or by handling objects. The word derives from the Greek *psyche* (soul) and *metron* (measure). Those skilled in psychometry may be able to pick up a random piece of jewelry and identify its wearer or owner. They may also be able to gather accurate information by simply shaking someone's hand. Someone possessing the power of psychometry may be able to assist in the solving of crimes by handling evidence found at a crime scene.

Those who are especially sensitive may be overwhelmed by the constant barrage of information. Everything they touch tells a story and reveals information. Wearing gloves may provide control over when and how much information is received. An example of this is seen in the second episode of the Japanese anime series, *Tokyo Babylon*.

Pyrokinesis

Pyrokinesis is the paranormal power to ignite and control fire. Pyrokinetics, people possessing the paranormal power of pyrokinesis, don't need matches. They can start fires with the power of their minds. Pyrokinetics are also known as fire starters. Some pyrokinetics, although not all, also have the power to extinguish fire.

Author Stephen King is credited with coining the term in his 1980 best-selling novel, *Firestarter*. The term derives from the Greek words *pyro* (fire) and *kinesis* (movement). It is an incomplete name, however. For example, telekinesis is the power to move objects using the mind, but not necessarily the power to make objects materialize. Those possessing pyrokinesis may be able to move and direct fire, but may also be able to create fire where it did not previously exist. Individual pyrokinetics may or may not be able to control and manipulate flames that they did not personally generate.

The most common form of pyrokinesis is the ability to ignite. Untrained pyrokinetics start fires without meaning to; intense emotions like anger or fear may simply trigger the process. Whatever they focus on may spontaneously burst into flame.

Pyrokinesis is not the same as spontaneous combustion. In general, spontaneous combustion victims did not demonstrate powers of pyrokinesis while alive. Spontaneous combustion is an example of some sort of internal flame that causes the victim—and typically *only* the victim, not his or her surroundings—to burst into unusually hot flames. Pyrokinesis is directed externally: pyrokinetics willingly or unwillingly start fires.

Unlike Marvel comic-book hero, Johnny Storm, the Human Torch, pyrokinetics are not immune to fire. They suffer burns and injuries just as they would with fire produced by any other means. However, a pyrokinetic with control over his or her skills will be able to direct fire as desired and extinguish it as needed. Another example of a fictional pyrokinetic is the Marvel comic-book character Pyro, who can manipulate and control flame, but cannot generate it. He carries a flame thrower in order to have access to fire at will.

In January 1882, the Michigan Medical News documented a case of pyrokinesis. After extensive testing, Dr.

L. C. Woodman proclaimed the powers of A. William Underwood of Paw Paw, Michigan to be authentic. Underwood, born circa 1855, could generate fire by breathing through a handkerchief held to his mouth while rubbing it vigorously with his hands. Within minutes, the handkerchief burst into flames and was consumed. Some debunkers not present at the scene insist that Underwood must have been concealing phosphorus in his mouth, however this assumes that the physician and other witnesses were in collusion with him.

Pyrokinesis is a particularly dangerous power and one that is crucial to control. Telepaths who lack control of their powers may accidentally "hear" what others really think of them. Those possessing powers of psychometry may have to wear gloves to prevent being overwhelmed by unsought information. Untrained pyrokinetics, on the other hand, start fires and injure others—often those they love. Pyrokinetics seeking to hone their skills should begin by mentally igniting and then extinguishing a single candle before *very* gradually increasing their targets.

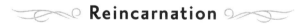 Reincarnation

The word *reincarnation* literally means "to be made flesh again." It refers to the belief that, after death, the soul enters another body and proceeds to live another life. Body, personality, circumstances, and even beliefs may vary from lifetime to lifetime, but the soul remains

constant and eternal. Reincarnation is a tenet of many religions, especially those of India (Hinduism, Jainism, Buddhism), as well as traditional Judaism. It is also incorporated into many New Age spiritual traditions.

Not all spiritual traditions interpret reincarnation in the same way. Some consider that the cycle of lifetimes is endless and eternal. Hinduism and Buddhism perceive reincarnation as a potentially finite cycle that offers the soul an opportunity to perfect itself. Karma earned in one lifetime affects the nature of future incarnations. The goal is eventually to depart this mortal coil by achieving nirvana (perfect enlightenment), which concludes the reincarnation cycle.

Some shamanic traditions believe that you always incarnate back into your own family. Thus your ancestors become your descendants. The belief that the soul may enter different species is known as *transmigration*, meaning that, although you are a human in this lifetime, you may be a tiger, insect, or bird in your next.

How can we reconcile reincarnation with the existence of ghosts? Each individual may have multiple souls that are bound together in life, but that separate from each other in death. Perhaps only one reincarnates. Alternatively, following death, some souls may fragment, leaving part of the soul as a ghost on Earth.

Reincarnation is a popular entertainment theme in novels, television, and films, including *The Mummy* starring Boris Karloff, *Dead Again*, and *Audrey Rose*.

Remote Viewing

Can you see what people a few miles away are eating for dinner? Can you describe the color of their tablecloth? If you are a remote viewer, you probably can. Remote viewing, also known as RV, is the ability to obtain information via paranormal means. Someone capable of remote viewing is able to see what is not visible. They are able to obtain information about things that are hidden from sight or are at such a great distance that they are impossible to see by regular means.

Roberts, Jane

Author, poet, and psychic Jane Roberts, born on May 8, 1929 in Saratoga Springs, New York, is most famous as the medium who channeled an entity named Seth. Her books *The Seth Material*, published in 1970, and *Seth Speaks*, published in 1972, were best-sellers that introduced the concept of channeling to a broad, general audience.

Roberts attended Skidmore College. In 1963, while researching extrasensory perception, Jane, together with her husband, Robert F. Butts, began to explore the spirit realm, contacting spirits via a Ouija board, automatic writing, and eventually automatic typing. On December 2, 1963, she encountered Seth, who defined himself as a "nonphysical entity."

Initially communicating through a Ouija board, Seth eventually communicated with Jane through clairaudience—in other words, she heard his messages in her head. Roberts eventually channeled Seth directly. According to Jane, Seth assumed control of her body while she was in a trance and spoke through her mouth, while her husband wrote down what was said. Some sessions were also recorded. Roberts held regular sessions with Seth for twenty-one years. Over sixteen books of Seth material are available. She was also the author of many other books, including *How to Develop Your ESP Power*. Roberts claimed to channel other spirits as well, including psychologist William James and artist Paul Cézanne.

Jane Roberts died on September 5, 1984 at fifty-five. Since her death, others have claimed to channel Seth (and Roberts); however, early in their communication, Seth advised that all true communication from him would be channeled by Roberts alone.

For more information, see *The Jane Roberts Papers*, an archive of her life and work housed at the Yale University Library that includes both published and unpublished writings, correspondence, journals, personal papers, and audio recordings of her channeling sessions; and *Speaking of Jane Roberts: Remembering the Author of the Seth Material,* by Susan M. Watkins, presents a literary portrait.

Roswell Incident

The Roswell Incident is the most famous UFO incident, bar none. Even those who know virtually nothing about UFOs are likely to be familiar with the name Roswell, and to know that *something* happened there. What they may not realize is that it did not actually happen in the town of Roswell itself.

Something crashed in the harsh, high desert near Corona, New Mexico. It is unclear exactly when the crash occurred, except that it took place in the first week of July 1947. Sometime that week, most likely on the night of July 3, an aircraft of unknown origin broke into a million little pieces over a sheep pasture in Corona, and over another site roughly twenty-five miles away. High winds whisked debris to the southeast for several days before authorities arrived to contain and clean up the sites. In 1947, this was an extremely remote region with little or no electricity and barely any telephone service. Roads were rough or nonexistent.

New Mexico wasn't just any old place. In 1947, it was the most highly guarded part of the United States. Roswell was the headquarters of the 509th Bomb Group—at that time, the only atomic strike force in the world. In 1945, the 509th had dropped atomic bombs on Hiroshima and Nagasaki. Dr. Robert Goddard (1882–1945), father of rocketry, worked in Roswell on secret rocket projects. Roswell also had interesting neighbors: the Trinity Site, where the very first nuclear device was detonated; Los Alamos, where the atomic bomb was created and where, in 1947, ongoing nuclear research was being conducted; and White Sands Proving Ground, where, in 1947, captured German V-2 rockets were being launched in the first phase of what would become the American space program.

It is unclear precisely when William W. "Mack" Brazel discovered that his pasture was covered with strange debris. Brazel was the foreman and custodian (not the owner, as is sometimes reported) of the J. B. Foster Ranch, located approximately thirty-three miles southeast of Corona. For several days, he consulted with his neighbors about what to do with all the debris. People flocked to take a look at what they believed to be the downed remains of a flying saucer and to collect pieces of debris.

Different types of debris were found. The most numerous were hand-sized or smaller fragments of something described as resembling the foil found within a pack of cigarettes, but very light and thin, and significantly stronger than expected. The debris allegedly included something now called "memory metal," which was thin, light, and aluminum-colored. When crumpled and placed on a flat surface, it un-crumpled itself, returning to its original, pristine condition with nary a crease or wrinkle. It could not be burned, scratched, or permanently damaged, although people tried, some claiming to shoot holes through it only to see the holes repair themselves spontaneously.

Debris that resembled I-beams or balsa-wood struts marked with strange symbols that some interpreted as "alien writing" were also found. These were described as bearing Egyptian-like hieroglyphs, although without the recognizable animal imagery typical of the Egyptians. Countless local ranchers and their families, including young children, investigated the crash sites before the military arrived days later.

Before he notified the military, Brazel tried to clean the pasture himself. He had cleaned up downed weather balloons before, as had other ranchers. Sheep, like goats, will consume anything, and Brazel was afraid they would eat the mysterious debris and be harmed. He discovered that this was not a problem, as his sheep adamantly refused to enter the pasture containing the debris—but this led to another complication. The sheep had to pass through this field to reach a source of water. The sheep were Brazel's responsibility, and he worried that they would become dehydrated in the summer heat.

Brazel was frustrated. There was a lot of debris to clean up—nearly a mile-long swath—and no evidence indicating who was responsible. There were no nametags or other markers. Nor was there information as to who should be notified of the crash—unlike weather research balloons, especially Project Mogul balloons, which instructed those who discovered them to contact New York University.

On Sunday morning, July 6, Brazel completed his weekly chores before driving seventy-five miles in his ancient pickup truck to Roswell to try to report the situation to someone in authority and in a position to help. (He may also have heard of a possible reward for anyone providing proof of a flying saucer.) He filled a couple of cardboard boxes with debris to show the authorities. Brazel first spoke to the local sheriff's office and to a Roswell radio station. They suggested he contact the Air Force, which he did. The Air Force took Brazel into custody and interrogated him. He was detained for several days during the clean-up operation.

On Monday, July 7, two intelligence officers from Roswell Army Air Force Base spent the day examining and collecting debris and containing the field. By nightfall, an area equivalent to a football field was still covered with debris. Fifty to sixty troops arrived on Tuesday for a full-scale cleanup. Extreme security measures were taken during the cleanup at the Foster Ranch, as well as at other locations. Armed guards encircled the primary areas, while a second cordon ringed the outer perimeter.

Sharpshooters assembled on surrounding hilltops and military police guarded roads leading to the sites. The military cleanup took over two days. During the cleanup, unscheduled flights arrived from Washington, D.C. and White Sands Army Air Force Base.

The military attempted to collect *all* debris. Neighbors, including children, had been collecting pieces. Local ranch houses were searched aggressively—without search warrants. The wooden floorboards of livestock sheds were pried loose. People claim that the military intimidated and threatened witnesses, including children, warning them never to discuss what they had seen.

On July 8, 1947, the *Roswell Daily Record's* headline proclaimed that the remains of a crashed alien spacecraft had been recovered on a ranch northeast of Roswell. At 11 A.M., Roswell Army Air Field Commanding Officer, Colonel William Blanchard, announced that a flying disc had been recovered. Several hours later, at approximately 4:30 in the afternoon, General Roger M. Ramey, commander of the Eighth Air Force and Blanchard's supervisor, presented an alternative scenario. Ramey announced to the press that, in fact, it was not a "flying disk," but a weather balloon. How did Blanchard make such a mistake? He was no neophyte, but the officer entrusted with oversight of the first atomic strike force.

Debris from Roswell was flown to U.S. Eighth Air Force headquarters in Fort Worth, Texas in a B-29

Superfortress bomber similar to the *Enola Gay*, the plane that dropped the atomic bomb on Hiroshima. This plane was operated by the 509th Bomb Group, the only unit on Earth then equipped to deliver atomic weapons. Only in Fort Worth was the debris discovered to be the remnants of a weather balloon.

Among those who misidentified this weather balloon were Brazel and his neighbors, who habitually cleaned up weather-balloon debris all by themselves without notifying authorities, members of the Roswell sheriff's department, and U.S. military intelligence personnel, who had authorized the military cleanup.

If it wasn't a UFO, then what was so significant that it required such a massive and secretive cover-up? What crashed? Roswell was an extremely remote region. Yet something so significant happened there that crowds traveled on horseback or by pickup truck to take a look at a pasture. And they brought their children to see it. Mack Brazel was not the only observer. Virtually all the local people came. Why? To see a weather balloon? There were many downed weather balloons in the region; they were not worthy of gossip or attention.

There are many theories as to what crashed near Roswell. Some suggest that it was some sort of highly classified experimental craft or a test rocket carrying monkeys. Perhaps it was a Japanese Fugo balloon-borne bomb, which were known to have traveled as far as Texas.

Rumors suggest that more than spaceship debris was discovered. A number of witnesses, both civilian and military, claim that there was a survivor of the crash. Allegedly, four aliens—three dead and one living—were found north of Roswell.

In 1993, responding to a request from New Mexico Congressman Steven Schiff, the Government Accounting Office (GAO), the investigative arm of the United States Congress, initiated and conducted a search of all relevant government agencies for documents regarding the Roswell incident. In 1995, the results were published, resulting in an even bigger mystery. *No* additional documents turned up beyond those already known. In addition, the GAO revealed that all other documents emanating from the Roswell Army Air Field covering the general time frame of the incident—including telexes, teletype messages, letters, correspondence, radio programs, and invoices—had been destroyed years earlier with no explanation or evident authority.

The town of Roswell and its very name are now synonymous with UFOs and extraterrestrials. UFOs drive the local economy in the same manner that witches drive the economy of Salem, Massachusetts. An annual UFO festival is held in Roswell in July. The city invites UFO enthusiasts and skeptics alike. Museums, stores, and restaurants are devoted to aliens. The television series *Roswell* and the *Roswell High* book series on which it is based are devoted to the premise that there were survivors of the 1947 crash.

Séance

A séance is a ritual for the purpose of summoning and communicating with spirits. The word derives from the French *seoir*, "to sit," because the standard séance involves a group of people sitting around a table. A synonym for *séance* is "a sitting." Participants are called "sitters."

There are many styles of séances. Modern Spiritualist séances may or may not incorporate the singing of hymns. A séance is typically led by a medium. There are usually between four and twelve participants who may be asked to sit in alternating male and female configuration. However, any organized ritual by which a medium contacts spirits for a client who is also present can be described as a séance. The creation of spirit photographs and precipitated spirit paintings are also classified as séances.

Although séances are associated with Spiritualism and Spiritism, it is an ancient concept shared by many cultures. The Bible's Medium of Endor essentially conducts a séance, even though that word is not used.

She summons the spirit of the prophet Samuel, as requested by her client, King Saul. She then facilitates communication between Saul, the sitter, and the ghost of Samuel. Visual examples of more or less realistic séances are found in films like *The Others*, *Séance on a Wet Afternoon*, and Fellini's *Juliet of the Spirits*.

Second Sight

Second sight is a Scottish term that is synonymous with clairvoyance and precognition. It is sometimes ominously called just "the sight." Second sight may be genetic, as it has a tendency to run in families. It is usually understood as a vision of what is destined to occur; however those gifted with the second sight may be sensitive to all sorts of paranormal or psychic activity.

Second sight is often perceived as a curse, as these visions tend to be of death or disaster, rather than of happy occasions. Second sight is involuntary, although those possessing it may be able to refine and expand their skills. There is a traditional belief that second sight is a spirit-initiated activity. In other words, a spirit actually bestows the visions that a person witnesses.

Shadow People or Shadow Beings

You see dark shadowy beings out of the corner of your eye, but when you swivel your head to get a better look, they vanish. Except sometimes, they don't. These dark, shadowy apparitions are known as shadow people, shadow folk, or shadow beings. Unlike the standard ghostly white apparition, shadow people are typically black or very dark apparitions. Despite their name, they are not always shadowy, but may also appear solid, smoky, or like dark mist. It is not entirely clear what they are. Shadow people may or may not be ghosts. Some ghost hunters insist that shadow people are a different kind of spirit, and they are sometimes described as "spirit shadows."

Shadow people lurk in shadows and corners, sometimes stepping out. Although they are usually

witnessed only with peripheral vision, sometimes they enter directly into a viewer's line of sight and linger, as if *they* were viewing *you*. Nothing reported indicates that shadow people cause harm; however their presence tends to instill a sense of foreboding and anxiety almost akin to the soul-eating Dementors of the Harry Potter universe.

Shadow people are reported quite frequently, and are apparently not uncommon. There are discrepancies among descriptions, however, and it is unclear whether all reports describe the same sort of entity. Some are humanoid in appearance, although few other details are offered. Shadow people are occasionally described as having glowing red or yellow eyes. They may manifest unusual movement and are sometimes described as appearing to be "liquid." A shadow man is allegedly in residence at the haunted prison in Moundsville, West Virginia.

Society for Psychical Research (SPR)

The Society for Psychical Research is a nonprofit organization founded in Great Britain in 1882 for the purpose of advancing the understanding of abilities and events commonly described as "paranormal" or "psychic." Founders include philosophers Henry Sidgwick and William Barrett, journalist Edmund Dawson Rogers, poet and psychologist Edward Gurney, and William Henry Myers, professor of physics at the Royal College of Science. The SPR publishes the quarterly *Journal of the Society for Psychical Research* and sponsors an annual conference as well as lectures throughout the year.

Its sister branch, The American Society for Psychical Research (ASPR), was founded in 1885 and is the oldest psychical research organization in the

United States. William James, the prominent psychologist, was among its founding members.

Sphinx

The Great Sphinx is a huge statue of a recumbent lion with a human head located near the pyramids of Giza. The sphinx is the largest monolith statue in the world, meaning that it is cut from a single block of stone. The Great Sphinx stands over sixty-six feet tall, and is approximately 241 feet long and twenty feet wide. Located on the west bank of the Nile near Cairo, Egypt's capital city, it is the oldest surviving monumental sculpture on Earth.

Sphinx is a Greek word that refers to a type of guardian spirit with the body of a lion and the head of another species, usually, but not always, human. The modern Egyptian Arabic name for this statue is *Abu al-Hul* or, in English, Father of Terror. What the ancient Egyptians called it is now unknown.

The Great Sphinx was buried in sand for centuries, until French explorers dug it up. However, it wasn't completely excavated until between 1925 and 1936. The Great Sphinx has been the subject of extensive research, but important questions remain. What is its origin? What is its purpose? Exactly how old is the Great Sphinx?

The conventional explanation suggests that it was built 4,600 years ago as a memorial to Pharaoh

Chefren, son of Pharaoh Cheops, builder of the neighboring Great Pyramid. However, some Egyptologists claim the sphinx is actually older than the pyramids and was built at least 12,000 years ago.

The sphinx's body (but not its head) shows signs of water erosion. French mathematician R. A. Schwaller published a paper in the 1930s arguing that the sphinx is older than commonly accepted based on water markings around it base. There was insufficient moisture in the Egyptian climate following 10,000 B.C.E. to account for this scale of water damage, he claimed; therefore it must have been built prior to that time. Those who disagree argue that this  erosion was caused by wind or sand, not by water. A counterargument then asks, why don't other structures dated to the Old Kingdom and built at approximately the same time and from the same limestone demonstrate the same type of erosion? The weathering displayed by the sphinx was caused by thousands of years of heavy rainfall, they argue.

Another mystery is who built the Great Sphinx? Is pharaonic Egyptian civilization more ancient than commonly accepted or is a now-unknown earlier civilization responsible? If so, were they survivors from Atlantis or even extraterrestrial visitors?

Spirit Board

A spirit board is a portal that allegedly allows living people to communicate with beings from other dimensions—most famously spirits of the dead, although other types of spirits may also be contacted. Some of the earliest contactees claim to have used spirit boards to converse with extraterrestrials. Spirit boards are also known as talking boards or witch boards but the most famous spirit board is the trademarked Ouija board (pronounced *wee-jee*). For many, it is the only familiar type of spirit board. Ouija has become synonymous with an entire genre of occult tools—just as the term "Scotch tape" is used to refer to any clear adhesive tape regardless of manufacturer. An example of a non-Ouija spirit board is featured on the television series *Charmed*.

The concept of communicating with spirits is eternal; however the industrial age changed the way people considered communication tools and devices. Samuel Morse's telegraph went into operation in 1844. A spirit board can be understood as the equivalent of a spiritual telegraph system. The spirit board made its American debut in 1880. Although most boards are now mass produced, the earliest models were homemade. Between 1890 and 1950, dozens of different manufacturers produced variations of the spirit board, with the Ouija board dominating the market.

Most spirit boards involve two pieces: the board itself and an accompanying planchette. The standard spirit board is a smooth, flat, usually rectangular board with the alphabet arranged across it, usually in two curving lines. Below the letters are the numbers from one through nine and zero. Entire words may also be featured on the board—usually "yes," "no," and "good-bye," but there may be variations.

The planchette is a small rolling pointer that slides easily across the board. It features a hole or window through which the letters and numbers can be read. *Planchette* literally means "little plank" and is named after a forerunner to the spirit board, a once popular device used for similar spirit-communication purposes. The modern planchette that accompanies a spirit board is a miniature version of the original device. Some people prefer a pendulum to the traditional planchette when using a spirit board.

To use the board, two people usually sit facing each other with the board between them, either on their knees or on a table. They place the planchette in its starting position in the center of the board and lightly rest their fingertips on it. Ideally, the planchette then begins to glide over the board, stopping and starting. As it stops over words, letters, and numbers, messages may form, either spontaneously or in response to questions.

The planchette allegedly moves of its

own volition, not because either of the participants is pushing it—or at least not consciously. Unconscious movement may be a mediumistic act, similar to automatic writing or channeling.

A standard opening question might be something like: "Is any spirit here?" If the answer is affirmative, then attempts are made to identify the spirit's identity. Messages may be received from loved ones, or strange, unknown spirits may manifest. Although sold in toy stores alongside board games, spirit boards are genuine medium's tools and should not be treated casually. Those who use them to taunt spirits or who mockingly summon demons often find that what they have really summoned is trouble—sometimes, trouble that may require a paranormal professional to remedy and clean up. Mediums and psychics who use spirit boards usually utilize protective rituals or devices to ensure safety, including protective circles, incense, amulets, or wards. Sometimes they ask protective spirits to serve as gatekeepers, ensuring that only benevolent spirits are permitted entry.

Any spirit that suggests causing harm to anyone— including yourself—is by definition a harmful spirit and should be banished. Deceased loved ones may mean well, but may not be any wiser in the afterlife than when they were alive. In other words, if Grandma Sue's career advice over the telephone was lousy when she was living, it may not be any better now that she is dead and communicating through a spirit board. Just because advice or information comes via a spirit board doesn't mean that it must be followed. If something scary manifests through the spirit board, the easiest way to close the portal is to put the board away.

For more information, go to The Museum of Talking Boards (*www.museumoftalkingboards.com*).

For more information on Ouija boards, go to *www.williamfuld.com*.

Spirit Cabinet

A spirit cabinet is an enclosure in which a medium is secluded during a séance. It is typically a wooden box, reminiscent of a Roman Catholic confessional booth and not dissimilar to the cabinets commonly used as stage magicians' props. However, a spirit cabinet may not actually be a cabinet; a curtained-off corner of a room is sometimes sufficient. In the mid 1850s, the Davenport brothers, a team of mediums, pioneered the use of the spirit cabinet during séances, integrating its role into modern Spiritualism.

Not all mediums use spirit cabinets. It is a matter of personal preference. Various reasons are given for employing one. Some claim that it protects the medium while he or she enters a trance state and may be considered a security device for mediums who produce ectoplasm, since contact with the medium during this process, or even exposure to bright light, may be harmful to the medium. The spirit cabinet has also been

described as a kind of spiritual storage battery or generator. Some mediums use cabinets to condense energy, which enables them to manifest spirits better. The privacy of the spirit cabinet, however, may also facilitate fraud.

Alternatively, spirit cabinets are used in attempts to prove that a physical medium cannot possibly be fraudulent. (These attempts may or may not also be fraudulent.) A medium may be bound hand and foot inside a cabinet, or otherwise incapacitated, to prove that spirits, not the medium, are producing the perceived phenomena. An example of a spirit cabinet is found in Mike Mignola's 2009 comic-book mini-series *Witchfinder: In the Service of Angels.*

Spirit Photography

Can a ghost be photographed? If a ghost is present, even if you can't see it with your eyes, will it be visible in a photograph? Spirit photography is an attempt to capture the images of ghosts photographically, in the same manner that EVP attempts to capture their voices in recordings. Spirit photography was once extremely popular throughout North America and the United Kingdom. Thousands of photographs were taken. Spirit photography also encompasses photographs taken during séances, many displaying images of ectoplasm.

The very first official example was displayed at the American Photographic Society in 1860. Photographer W. Campbell of Jersey City took a test photo of an empty chair in his studio. When it was developed, however, it showed the image of a young boy seated on the chair. Campbell was never able to produce any other spirit photographs.

The first professional spirit photographer is generally considered to be William Mumler, who produced his first spirit photograph in 1861 by accident. He continued to create these photographs throughout his career. Photography was a new art. People were captivated by the concept of possessing an image of someone they loved, especially when that loved one was absent. People flocked to photo studios. Photographers were summoned to capture images of the dead before they were interred. These were known as mourning photographs and an example appears in the Nicole Kidman film, *The Others*.

But what of people who died before photography was invented? Spirit photographers claimed to be able to capture images of those who were already dead. Spirit photography was controversial from its beginnings. Are spirit photographs genuine or are they tricks? Only professionals owned photographic equipment in those days, so the person taking the spirit photo played a dual role: photographer and medium. As mediums, they summoned a spirit; as photographers, they captured that spirit's image. Unlike many other mediums, spirit photographers charged substantial fees for their services. It was a lucrative business, furthering suspicion of fraud. The general consensus now is that many spirit photographs were faked, but there are some spirit photos extant for which no conventional explanation exists.

Not all spirit photographs are identical or of the same quality. Usually ghosts appear to be transpar-

ent or misty. They may be draped in white fabric or sheets. They may appear as fully formed spirits, or only ghostly faces may appear.

How are spirit photographs produced? The camera may serve as a medium, enabling spirits to communicate or manifest. Some theorize that it is the effect of some sort of ghost-derived radiation on photosensitive film. Alternatively, it may be a result of the conscious or unconscious rapport of the photographer with spirits. The photographic sitting may be understood as a form of séance.

Primitive cameras demanded that a sitter remain very still for an extended period of time while the shutter remained open. It was not difficult for a photographer's assistant dressed as a ghost to slip silently behind a sitter and then depart unnoticed. The use of heavy drapes and curtains in photo studios also facilitated fraud. Fraudulent spirit photographs can also be created by superimposing ghostly images and double exposures, as well as by using sleight of hand to replace actual photos.

Even many of the obviously fraudulent photos are very beautiful, however, and are now appreciated as a form of performance art. In 2005, a wide selection of evocative, haunting spirit photographs were a featured exhibition at New York City's Metropolitan Museum of Art (*The Perfect Medium: Photography and the Occult*).

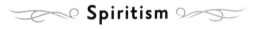

Spiritism

A medium told Frenchman Hypolite Leon Denizard Rivail (October 3, 1804–March 31, 1869) that he had been a Druid named Allan in a previous lifetime. Another medium told him he had been named Kardec or Kardek in another previous life. Rivail thus adopted the name Allan Kardec and became the father of the spiritual system known as Spiritism.

Spiritism is not a misspelling of Spiritualism. It is a different, albeit related, tradition that first developed in France, but became extremely popular and influential in Latin America and the Philippines. The Spanish form of the name is *Espiritismo*. In Brazil, Spiritism is known as *Kardecismo*. Camille Flammarion (1842–1925), the French astronomer, described Spiritism as a science, not a religion.

Kardec was a teacher (physics, chemistry, anatomy, physiology, astronomy, and math) who organized and taught free classes for the poor when he became fascinated with Spiritualism. When news about the Rochester Rappers reached France, Kardec decided to investigate for himself, and so began to consult mediums and attend séances. What he discovered enthralled him. Kardec worked closely with several mediums. Through them, he acquired a vast body of knowledge regarding the progression of the human soul. He organized and published the information, and his books became best-sellers, especially in Latin America. Spiritism is based on the five books of Kardec.

Spiritism espouses reincarnation, a belief not necessarily shared by Spiritualists. Inscribed over Kardec's tomb at Père Lachaise cemetery in Paris are the words: "To be born, to die, to be reborn again and so progress unceasingly, that is the law." This phrase is now considered among the chief tenets of Spiritism. Kardec, unlike many Spiritualists, was not interested in physical mediumship, only in message mediumship.

Another tenet of Spiritism is that charity is essential to salvation, and that the highest form of charity is the gift of health. Thus psychic healing is an extremely important aspect of Spiritism. In Brazil, there are Spiritist hospitals where physicians work side-by-side with mediums. Palmelo, a Spiritist community in Brazil, was founded in 1925. For more information, see Allan Kardec's *The Book on Mediums: Guide for Mediums and Invocators*, now available in English translation.

Spiritualism

Spiritualism is not a synonym for "spiritual." It names a spiritual tradition variously understood as a philosophy, a practice, a science, and/or a religion. Spiritualism is a distinct religion, not a branch of Christianity or any other faith. A Spiritualist is someone who believes, as the basis of her or his religion, in the immortality of the soul. The individual human personality somehow survives the death of the body. Death is a transition, not an end. Life does not terminate at death, but is continuous, as demonstrated by communication between the realms of the living and the dead, facilitated by mediums. Some, but not all, Spiritualists are mediums. Not all mediums are Spiritualists.

March 31, 1848 is traditionally considered the birth of the modern Spiritualist movement, as that is when the young Fox sisters allegedly made contact with the spirit of a murdered peddler whose remains were hidden in their home in Hydesville, New York. By the spring of 1852, there were reputedly 40,000 devotees of Spiritualism in New York City alone. It is estimated that, in 1854, somewhere between one and two million Americans were active Spiritualists.

The birth of Spiritualism coincided with the introduction of many then-revolutionary inventions involving communication, including the telegraph and the telephone. For many, the boundaries of communication appeared limitless. If people could now speak to each other over long distances via a machine, why shouldn't they also be able to speak with the dead? For Spiritualists, conversations with the dead are not miracles, but everyday occurrences.

Spiritualism was very controversial. Some associated it with "devil worship." Many Spiritualist mediums experienced extreme hostility, like the assassination plot against Maggie Fox. After New York State Supreme Court Judge John Worth Edmonds (1816–1874) published his book *Spiritualism* in 1853, outrage by his colleagues forced him to resign from the bench. On November 3, 1893, Spiritualists, frustrated with constant accusations of fraud and also with charlatans pretending to be true mediums, founded the National Spiritualist Association of Churches (NSAC), a nonprofit religious organization. The organization now includes approximately 150 Spiritualist churches under its charter.

Famous Spiritualists and enthusiasts include artists James Whistler, Dante Gabriel Rossetti, and Edvard Munch, famous for his painting *The Scream*; author Sir Arthur Conan Doyle; Isaac Funk, publisher of Funk and Wagnall's reference books; and poets Alfred Lord Tennyson and Christina Rossetti.

Spontaneous Combustion

How does a human body catch fire for no apparent reason? Spontaneous combustion occurs when something or someone burns with no identifiable ignition source. Also known as Spontaneous Human Combustion (SHC), hundreds of cases have been reported, with medical records of the events dating back to the 17th century. Most remain unsolved mysteries.

Spontaneous combustion involves odd, mysterious fires. It is characterized by heat so intense that the body is cremated, leaving behind only a pile of ashes. In general, only the person who has combusted is burned. Their surroundings may remain completely untouched by fire, or merely mildly singed. The fire seems to come from within the body, not from an external source. It also seems to burn out as soon as its source is destroyed.

Many, but not all, victims were drinking heavily prior to their combustion, leading some to theorize that alcohol is a factor. Another theory blames static electricity. Some individuals generate up to 30,000 volts of static electricity, ordinarily discharged through hair. Some scientists think that, given the right circumstances, gases within the body may ignite. Alternatively, some unknown agent within the body—again, possibly a gas—may be responsible for triggering combustion. A fictional example of spontaneous combustion occurs in Charles Dickens' novel, *Bleak House*.

Stone Tape Theory

Are all ghosts independent sentient entities, or is there another explanation for hauntings? Stone Tape Theory is a mystical concept that demystifies ghosts. Also known as residual haunting, energy remnants, and memory imprints, the theory suggests that intense human emotions can somehow become imprinted into stones, bricks, crystals, fabric, or landscapes in such a way that the image of the person transmitting those emotions is played back periodically in the manner of a tape recording. These images may be witnessed by others and understood as ghosts or phantoms. Thus, although they are interpreted as "ghosts," they are really only remnants or vestiges of an event that has somehow become imprinted on its surroundings.

Stone Tape Theory does not deny the existence of ghosts. Hypothetically, a house can possess both residual haunting and real ghosts. Ghosts associated with residual hauntings are characterized by specific types of

behavior. They act like recordings. The same apparition appears at the same time in the same place doing the same thing almost as if on schedule. Evidence indicates that these entities are not interactive and may not be intelligent. Ghosts associated with Stone Tape Theory tend not to respond to observers, but simply repeat a series of actions before vanishing. They are frightening because of their presence and behavior, but do not actually harm anyone. An example is a ghost that continually reappears at a crime scene, precisely repeating the exact same actions.

Stone Tape Theory ghosts tend to be linked to specific places or objects. Residual hauntings naturally occur in extreme situations accompanied by intense emotions like terror. They are based on two components. First, information may be imbedded in material. There is an ancient metaphysical theory that stones, crystals, and mirrors retain information and impressions that can be accessed later by those who know how. Second, the ability to experience a haunting may depend on a beholder's sensitivity. The more sensitive will see or hear the phenomena with greater clarity, while others may essentially receive no "playback." In other words, if a tree falls in a forest and no one is there to hear it, does it make a sound? If a ghost haunts a room, but no one can see it, is it really there? Stone Tape Theory suggests that most hauntings go unperceived.

This is a controversial theory. How Stone Tape Theory actually works—why some events are imprinted,

but not others—is unknown. The official origins of the theory date back to a 1972 BBC Christmas broadcast called *The Stone Tape*, starring Jane Asher and Michael Bryant, and written by English science-fiction great, Nigel Kneale. In the film, a team of corporate researchers seeking new technology set up headquarters in a Victorian mansion and discover that it is haunted. Some of the researchers, in particular the Jane Asher character, are able to see *and* hear the ghost vividly. Others can only see *or* hear it. Some can feel the temperature drop whenever the haunting phenomenon begins. One man is entirely oblivious, although he acknowledges the validity of what others experience. It is finally discovered that the haunting is being produced by a "recording" imbedded in the stone in one room.

Synchronicity

One afternoon, for no apparent reason, Susan suddenly thought of Mary, an old college friend she hadn't seen or heard from in years. Simultaneously, Susan's mail arrived, bringing with it a totally unexpected letter from Mary. Coincidence? Some might think so. Others would call it synchronicity.

Synchronicity is the name of a philosophical concept that identifies situations in which two or more events occur simultaneously although they are apparently causally unrelated. In other words, these events seem to have nothing in common beyond the fact that they occurred simultaneously. It is the theory of the greater significance of coincidences. This concept was first described by the pioneering psychiatrist Carl Jung (1875–1961), who described synchronicity as "meaningful coincidence." Jung theorized that specific moments in time possess unique and significant qualities. Thus, anything occurring at a fixed moment of time shares the essence of that particular moment. Jung believed that synchronicity provides the bridge between science, religion, and the paranormal.

In his 1952 book *Synchronicity: An Acausal Connecting Principle*, Jung described the pivotal experience that brought this concept to his attention. He was in his Swiss office with one of his patients, a young woman, who was describing a dream in which she had received a golden scarab. Meanwhile, Jung was sitting with his back to a closed window. Hearing a tapping sound behind him, he turned and saw a flying insect knocking against the glass from the outside. Jung opened the window and captured the creature as it entered the room. It was a rose-chafer or, as he described it, a "scarabaeid beetle," the closest thing to a golden scarab to be found naturally in Switzerland. This rose-chafer had, contrary to its usual nature, felt compelled to enter that specific darkened room at that precise moment. Its appearance provided Jung with the key to interpreting this woman's dream.

Table Tapping

Any sort of table-related séance phenomena can be classified as table tapping, even if no literal tapping is involved. Is table tapping merely a parlor game, or is it proof of spirit activity and life everlasting?

This phenomenon, also known as table tipping, table knocking, table turning, or spirit rapping, first came to general attention with the Fox sisters and the birth of modern Spiritualism, but it has existed for centuries. The basic technique involves a small group of people, usually four or five, sitting around a table. All place their hands flat on the table surface. Eventually, some sort of phenomena should occur. The table may levitate or vibrate, or mysterious knocking or rapping sounds may emanate. Multiple sittings may be required before results are seen. It is usually advised that the same people be present at all sittings.

Telekinesis

Also known as psychokinesis (PK), telekinesis (TK) is the paranormal ability to move objects without actually touching them, using only the power of the mind. The term *telekinesis* was first coined in 1890. Physical mediums may demonstrate telekinesis during séances. Levitating a table during a séance is considered a form of telekinesis.

Telekinesis is a popular theme in entertainment fiction, notably in the 1952 novella by Jack Vance, *Telek*. Among the many comic superheroes manifesting telekinetic powers are Jean Grey, Cable, Psylocke, and Hellion.

Telepathy

Can you accurately read the thoughts of others? Can two people conduct a conversation silently, using only the power of their minds? Telepaths can allegedly do just that. A telepath can hear the silent thoughts of others as if they were spoken aloud. Theoretically, two or more telepaths brought together may be able to communicate with each other in complete silence.

The term *telepathy* was coined by the Society for Psychical Research in 1882. Previously, this skill was known as *thought transference*. Sigmund Freud believed that telepathy was possible when he noticed that analysts and their patients often seemed to pick up each other's thoughts. As with other extrasensory skills—for instance, clairvoyance or clairaudience—not all telepaths function in precisely the same manner. Some have more control over their powers than others. Some people may experience telepathy as occasional, uncontrolled experiences, while others are able to turn this ability off and on at will.

Pulitzer Prize winning author and muckraker, Upton Sinclair (1878–1968), most famous for his novel *The Jungle*, chronicled experiments in telepathy conducted by himself and his wife, Mary Craig, in his 1930 book *Mental Radio*. Sinclair sat at a desk in one room, drew a picture, and brought it to Mary, who was reclining in another room. Without looking at his picture, she placed it face down on her solar plexus, received a mental impression, then reproduced it. *Mental Radio* reproduces some of their drawings and records 210 successful experiments. The book was originally self-published, as Sinclair could find no publisher willing to take it on. A publisher eventually put out an edition, and *Mental Radio* remains in print to this day. Albert Einstein wrote the forward to the German translation.

Transgenic Beings

Back in 1961, when Betty and Barney Hill were allegedly abducted by aliens, most people hearing of genetic and reproductive engineering would have considered it fantasy or science fiction—just as strange and unrealistic as extraterrestrials and flying saucers. Today, of course, reproductive technology is a thriving science and business.

Many abductees, beginning with the Hills, report that aliens harvested their genetic material (their ova or sperm). Some have even reported the premature removal of viable fetuses, as late as the seventh month of pregnancy. Why?

Back when the first abductees came forward with these claims, they were dismissed as nonsense. That was before reproductive technology and transgenic species existed. Transgenic plants and animals are created in laboratories by transferring genes from one species to another. For example, regular mice cannot be infected with polio. However, mice that have received the human gene for the polio receptor can contract the disease and be used in laboratory experiments. This is fairly new technology for humans. Is it possible that technologically advanced aliens possessed this knowledge long before we did?

Based on descriptions of them, it is unlikely that aliens could blend seamlessly into human society. They cannot lurk incognito. One theory suggests that extraterrestrials are creating transgenic offspring that may appear physically indistinguishable from humans, while secretly serving their alien masters. These non-human beings may already live among us.

UFO

UFO is an acronym for Unidentified Flying Object. Hypothetically speaking, that's all a UFO is: something flying in the sky that cannot be identified. However, in the 21st century, UFO is generally understood to be a synonym for an aircraft of extraterrestrial origin. Some people who acknowledge the existence of UFOs resent this assumption of extraterrestrial origin, suggesting

that UFOs may also be unknown military or surveillance aircraft.

Reports of strange flying objects in the sky are nothing new, although interpretations have evolved over the ages. In mythology, deities of many cultures are described as traveling in celestial chariots. Aphrodite's flying chariot is pulled by doves, while Thor's is pulled by goats. The Bible records several flying vehicles, including Ezekiel's flaming chariot and the chariot witnessed by the prophet Elisha that transported Elijah into the sky. In the 19th century, many astronomers and ship's captains described witnessing strange, unexplained phenomena.

Before the invention of the airplane, however, witnessed unidentified flying objects could not be interpreted as aircraft, but were understood as spiritual or strange natural phenomenon. There was little, if any, concept of manufactured mechanical flight prior to the first exhibitions by the Wright Brothers in 1903, or at least none held by the general public. Not until 1911 to 1912 did planes appear with any regularity or in any number, and even then this occurred mainly at air shows. In those days, even if you saw something in the sky, would it ever occur to you that it might be a spaceship from a distant planet?

In the 1930s, reports of mystery airplanes proliferated and increased throughout North America and

Europe, coinciding with the cult of celebrity pilots like Charles Lindbergh and Amelia Earhart. People's expectations when they gazed heavenward had evolved. The first official sighting of a UFO is considered to have occurred on June 24, 1947 in North America's Pacific Northwest, where Kenneth Arnold (1915–1984), a veteran mountain pilot, was participating in a search for a lost military transport plane near Mount Rainier in the Cascade Mountains. (There was a $5,000 reward.)

Arnold saw something unusual glinting in the distance and went to investigate. What he saw appeared to be a formation of nine or more craft flying in a line around a series of mountain peaks. He considered and ruled out the possibility that they were geese. He clocked them and determined that they were flying at 1,700 miles per hour, a speed airplanes did not approach for another fifteen years. When Arnold landed in Yakima, he told the airport general manager what he had seen. The story spread and, by the next day, reporters contacted Arnold, who described the flight pattern of what he had seen as resembling that of a saucer that was skipped across water. The media transformed this into "flying saucers." Arnold always felt that he was misquoted, as he had been describing the crafts' motion, not their shape.

His was but the first of numerous reported sightings that summer, including many from highly qualified and credible observers like Air Force officers and commercial pilots. These craft were witnessed at high and low altitudes, and flying at high and low speeds. The reports peak around the July 4th weekend, coinciding with the incident at Roswell. Fewer reports occur after this period, although reports may have been suppressed in Roswell's wake.

Newspaper and radio accounts were filled with reports of UFOs, as well as explanations from scientists dismissing and explaining away what they hadn't personally witnessed or studied, something otherwise-reputable scientists would not do with other topics. UFOs were, and routinely are, ridiculed as nonsense. In his memoir, ufologist Budd Hopkins theorizes that the 1938 Orson Welles radio broadcast of H. G. Wells' *War of the Worlds*, which many mistook for a news report of a hostile Martian invasion, served to inoculate the general population against UFOs. Having been fooled once, people were reluctant to take a second chance.

UFO sightings are commonly dismissed as hallucinations, vivid imaginings, optical illusions, or indication of mental illness. Alternatively, observers may have confused airplanes, balloons, or planets for other craft. People have even been accused of mistaking large, flat hailstones for UFOs. It is estimated that 90 to 95 percent of all UFOs could be identified if only the right experts were able to see them. But what of that remaining 5 to 10 percent?

Many self-identified "UFO skeptics" resist acknowledging testimony by witnesses as "proof," although similar testimony would be sufficient proof in criminal cases, including death-penalty cases. Evidence like damage to trees, burns that resemble radiation burns, and depressions on the ground are inconclusive—they could, indeed, be attributed to something else. What would be incontrovertible is some sort of physical evidence that could be collected and analyzed by scientists—for example, a crashed aircraft or even a piece of one, or a downed crew member—hence the fascination with the Roswell incident.

X-Ray Vision

Someone possessing x-ray vision can literally undress you with his or her eyes. Also known as x-ray clairvoyance, x-ray vision is a form of clairvoyance in which one can see through physical objects or living beings. It may or may not be selective. A person possessing x-ray vision may or may not be able to control when or how this power is used. Not every case of x-ray vision is the same. One person with x-ray vision may be able to look at another person and see their underwear beneath their clothes, while another may see bones or internal organs. Others may be able to see through walls, sealed boxes, or envelopes.

Influential American Spiritualist Andrew Jackson Davis (1826–1910), known as the Poughkeepsie Seer, used what were known as his "spirit eyes" to heal. He said that he could see an individual's inner organs as if the body were transparent. Each organ stood out vividly and with a brightness that was diminished if disease was present. Superman is the most famous fictional character to possess x-ray vision.

Yeti

The *yeti* is a type of cryptid, also sometimes called the Abominable Snowman, that allegedly inhabits the Himalayas. Described as a hairy primate with human features, expressive eyes, and no tail, it is extremely tall, possibly as high as ten feet. Tales of similar large, shambling humanoid beings come from many mountain ranges in many distant places. These include the *meti* from the Gobi Desert; the *kang-mi* and *migo* from elsewhere in Asia; the Australian *yowee*; and, from North America, Sasquatch or Bigfoot. Reports of huge, wild hairy red men have circulated in the Pamir Mountains for centuries.

Traditional tales of the yeti were dismissed as "folklore" by Westerners. It was not until reports of sightings by Westerners that the existence of the yeti was taken seriously. The first reported sighting of the yeti by a Westerner occurred in 1889, when a British army major discovered a huge footprint that he associated with the folktales. In 1921, Lt. Colonel Charles Kenneth Howard-Bury, leader of a British army expedition, reported seeing yetis in nearby snowfields. Yeti sightings rapidly multiplied. In 1925, Soviet army troops allegedly shot one in self-defense. A series of photographs of alleged yeti footprints were published in 1951. They resembled human footprints, but were extraordinarily large.

No yeti has ever been captured, alive or dead, nor has there ever been conclusive evidence of its existence. Some believe that no yeti will ever be captured because it is a spirit being, not flesh and blood. Similar legends are told of Sasquatch. Alternatively, some believe the yeti to be an as-yet undiscovered species. Another theory suggests that the remote regions where these sightings occur enabled the survival of *Gigantopithecus*, a giant primate who existed from five million to a half million years ago.

Resource Guide

Books

Alexander, Steve and Karen. *Crop Circles: Signs, Wonders, and Mysteries.* London: Arcturus Publishing, 2008.

Aykroyd, Peter H. with Angela North. *A History of Ghosts: The True Story of Séances, Mediums, Ghosts, and Ghostbusters.* New York: Rodale, 2009.

Bryan, C. D. B. *Close Encounters of the Fourth Kind.* New York: Penguin Arkana, 1996.

Buckland, Raymond. *Buckland's Book of Spirit Communications.* St. Paul, MN: Llewellyn Publications, 2004.

Buckland, Raymond. *The Spirit Book: The Encyclopedia of Clairvoyance, Channeling, and Spirit Communication.* Canton, MI: Visible Ink Press, 2005.

Buckland, Raymond. *The Weiser Field Guide to Ghosts.* San Francisco: Red Wheel/Weiser, 2009.

Budd, Deena West. *The Weiser Field Guide to Cryptozoology.* San Francisco: Red Wheel/Weiser, 2010.

Carey, Thomas J., and Donald R. Schmidt. *Witness to Roswell.* Franklin Lakes, NJ: Career Press/New Page, 2009.

Cheroux, Clement, et al. *The Perfect Medium: Photography and the Occult.* New Haven: Yale University Press, 2005.

Cox, Robert. *Body and Soul: A Sympathetic History of American Spiritualism.* Charlottesville: University of Virginia Press, 2003.

Fort, Charles. *The Book of the Damned: The Collected Works of Charles Fort.* New York: Jeremy P. Tarcher/Penguin, 2008.

Friedman, Stanton C., and Kathleen Marden. *Captured! The Betty and Barney Hill UFO Experience.* Franklin Lakes, NJ: The Career Press, 2007.

Glickman, Michael. *Crop Circles: The Bones of God.* Berkeley, CA: Frog Books, 2009.

Hopkins, Budd. *Art, Life and UFOs.* San Antonio, TX: Anomalist Books, 2009.

Illes, Judika. *The Encyclopedia of Spirits*. San Francisco: HarperOne, 2008.

Jolly, Martyn. *Faces of the Living Dead: The Belief in Spirit Photography*. New York: Mark Batty Publisher, 2006.

Kaplan, Louis. *The Strange Case of William Mumler: Spirit Photographer*. Minneapolis: University of Minnesota Press, 2008.

Kardec, Allan. *The Book on Mediums: Guide for Mediums and Invocators*. York Beach, ME: Weiser Books, 2000.

Main, Roderick. *Jung on Synchronicity and the Paranormal*. Princeton, NJ: University of Princeton Press, 1997

Marsh, Clint. *The Mentalist's Handbook: An Explorer's Guide to Astral, Spirit, and Psychic Worlds*. San Francisco: Weiser Books, 2008.

Melchizedek, Drunvalo. *Serpent of Light*. San Francisco: Weiser Books, 2007.

Nagy, Ron. *Precipitated Spirit Paintings*. Lakeville, MN: Galde Press, 2006.

Paxson, Diana. *Trance-portation: Learning to Navigate the Inner World*. San Francisco: Weiser Books, 2008.

Steinmeyer, Jim. *Charles Fort: The Man Who Invented the Supernatural*. New York: Jeremy P. Tarcher/Penguin, 2008.

Stuart, Nancy Rubin. *The Reluctant Spiritualist: The Life of Maggie Fox*. Orlando: Harcourt, Inc. 2005.

Taylor, Troy. *Ghosts by Gaslight: The History and Mystery of the Spiritualists and the Ghost Hunters*. Decatur, IL: Whitechapel Productions, 2007.

Violini, Juanita Rose. *Almanac of the Infamous, The Incredible and the Ignored*. San Francisco: Weiser Books, 2009.

Watkins, Susan M. *Speaking of Jane Roberts: Remembering the Author of the Seth Material*. Portsmouth, NH: Moment Point Press, 2001.

Wicker, Christine. *Lily Dale: The True Story of the Town that Talks to the Dead*. San Francisco: HarperSanFrancisco, 2003.

Willin, Melvyn. *Ghosts Caught on Film*. Cincinnati: David & Charles, 2007.

Wilson, Colin, and Damon Wilson. *The Mammoth Encyclopedia of the Unsolved*. Philadelphia: Running Press Books, 2000.

Organizations

American Association of Electronic Voice Phenomena
(*www.aaevp.com*)

First Spiritualist Temple (*www.fst.org/about_fst.htm*)

Mutual UFO Network (MUFON) (*www.mufon.com*)

National Spiritualist Association of Churches (NSAC)
(*www.nsac.org*)

Project 1947 (*www.project1947.com*)

Periodicals

Fortean Times Magazine (*www.forteantimes.com*)

UFO Magazine (*www.ufomag.com*)

Venture Inward Magazine (*http://ventureinward.org*)

Places

A Guide to Haunted Places (*www.haunted-places-to-go.com/index.html*)

International UFO Museum and Research Center, Roswell, NM
(*www.roswellufomuseum.com*)

Lily Dale, including the Lily Dale Museum
(*www.lilydaleassembly.com*)

Wonewoc Spiritualist Camp (*www.campwonewoc.com/index.html*)

Websites

Amazing Crystal Skulls (*www.crystalskulls.com*)

Crop Circles (*www.cropcircleconnector.com*)

Dreamland Resort (*http://dreamlandresort.com*)

Ghost Village (*www.ghostvillage.com*)

Haunted Museum (*www.prairieghosts.com/museum.html*)

Museum of Talking Boards (*http://museumoftalkingboards.com*)

Parapsychic Research Cooperative (PARC) (*http://parc.web.fm*)

Phone Calls from the Dead (*www.phonecallsfromthedead.net*)

Roswell Files (*http://roswellfiles.com*)

Sons of T. C. Lethbridge (*www.tc-lethbridge.com/home*)

Survival after Death (*www.survivalafterdeath.org.uk/home.htm*)

Recordings

Ghost Orchid: An Introduction to EVP (Ash International and Parapsychic Research Cooperative)

Index of Terms

Credits

About the Author

Judith Joyce grew up in a family of Spiritualists, psychics, and prophetic dreamers. She has had a vigorous interest in the paranormal ever since.

To Our Readers

Weiser Books, an imprint of Red Wheel/Weiser, publishes books across the entire spectrum of occult and esoteric subjects. Our mission is to publish quality books that will make a difference in people's lives without advocating any one particular path or field of study. We value the integrity, originality, and depth of knowledge of our authors.

Our readers are our most important resource, and we appreciate your input, suggestions, and ideas about what you would like to see published. Please feel free to contact us to request our latest book catalog, or to be added to our mailing list.

Red Wheel/Weiser, LLC
500 Third Street, Suite 230
San Francisco, CA 94107
www.redwheelweiser.com